Praise for Healing Virtues

"Having read much of Kathleen's writing, communicated with her by email and phone and also spent an afternoon with her, I know she is someone who understands animals and has achieved an important level of wisdom in knowing how to share Reiki with them. Reading her manuscript on a code of ethics for animal Reiki practitioners is a healing experience in itself. Her writing takes the reader into the world of animal consciousness, which is free of much of the perplexing emotional turmoil that humans experience. Once in this state, one becomes aware of the simplicity and beauty of the animal world and can allow this special awareness to guide animal Reiki sessions. I highly recommend getting her new book and using the information to share Reiki with the animals you encounter in your life."

–William Lee Rand, founder and president of The International Center for Reiki Training (ICRT), The Center for Reiki Research and The Reiki Membership Association

D0556953

"To me, this book is not just a Code of Ethics intended for animal Reiki practitioners. This book contains spiritual teachings and guidelines for all Reiki practitioners. I am thankful to the author, Kathleen Prasad, for sharing with us her deep wisdom through animal Reiki practices."

—Hyakuten Inamoto, founder of Komyo ReikiDo

"Healing Virtues is another gem from Kathleen Prasad about the ethics of animal healing. Her book is divided into different sections, which not only help you to understand the specific ethic being discussed but also include specific meditations to help you to gain a direct experience of each ethic. I highly recommend this book for people who like to focus on animal Reiki."

—Frans Stiene, co-founder of The International House of Reiki and author of *The Inner Heart of Reiki: Rediscovering Your True Self* and Reiki Insights

HEALING
VIRTUES

Transforming Your Practice Through the
Animal Reiki Practitioner Code of Ethics

HEALING VIRTUES

Transforming Your Practice Through the
Animal Reiki Practitioner Code of Ethics

KATHLEEN PRASAD

Published in the United States by

Animal Reiki Source, San Rafael, CA

ISBN: 978-0-9983580-1-7

Production Design and Cover: www.Damonza.com

DISCLAIMER: The suggestions in this book are not intended as a substitute for professional veterinary care. Reiki sessions are given for the purpose of stress reduction and relaxation to promote healing. Reiki is not a substitute for medical diagnosis and treatment. Reiki practitioners do not diagnose conditions nor do they prescribe, perform medical treatment, nor interfere with the treatment of a licensed medical professional. It is recommended that animals be taken to a licensed veterinarian or licensed health care professional for any ailment they have.

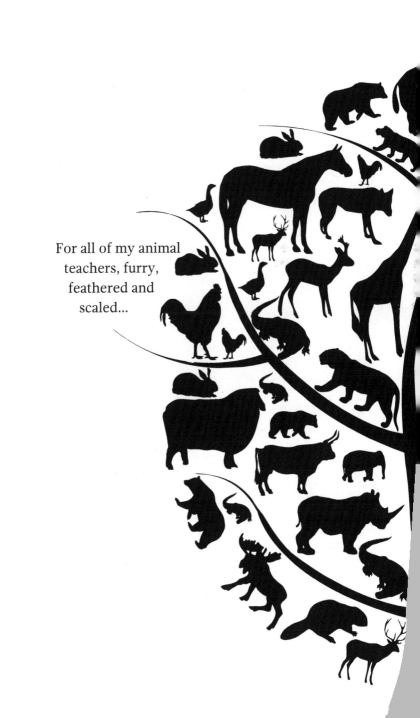

For all of my animal teachers, furry, feathered and scaled...

CONTENTS

How to Use This Book

Welcome to *The Healing Virtues: Transforming Your Practice Through the Animal Reiki Practitioner Code of Ethics*, an e-book and print book based on my tele-class of the same name. This book is meant as a professional reference for all levels of Reiki practitioners who are interested in learning the best ways to share Reiki with animals and their animal-loving community. It is an important source of information for Reiki teachers wishing to add Animal Reiki to their curriculum. This book can also be used as a resource for animal organizations and professionals who are interested in adding Reiki to their healing programs: sharing this book with resident Reiki practitioners can ensure that everyone is on the same page with approach and intent. Above all, this book is meant to expand compassion and protect and honor all animals and their people through the oftentimes complex and always beautiful journey of healing.

I'm really excited to be sharing the Animal Reiki Practitioner Code of Ethics with you in this book. It's been 10 years since I wrote this code and I'm very happy to say that when I read through it now, having had 10 more years of experience in my own practice of treatments and teaching classes and learning from animals, I still feel very proud of what I wrote. I feel that it is very complete and it is still totally in line with my work in this field. It's almost as if there were angel animals watching over me as I was writing it 10 years ago saying, "We've gotta make this last the long haul." When I look back to those days, it was very different from what it is today as far as how many practitioners there are and the current amount of knowledge and acceptance of Reiki. Reiki for animals is much more accepted today than it was 10 years ago.

This book is divided into a series of lessons. In each lesson, we will go over each section of the code of ethics in depth and I will also share a meditation on that section. I want us to look at each section of the code beyond just reciting it because you might read through it once and then not look at it again. It's most powerful when we really can contemplate and meditate on it. That is my goal for the time that we spend together through this book—that you look at each section of the code of ethics on its own and think about how it might improve the way that you offer Reiki to animals and their people in the future. The meditations are intended to support you to create both a powerful and ethically guided "Reiki space" of healing for the animals in your life!

Purpose and Guiding Principles

In this first lesson, I will be sharing with you the guiding principles of the code, and in so doing help to clarify your own goals for your practice.

Purpose

I am going to start with a very basic question: Why write a code of ethics for Animal Reiki practitioners anyway? First and foremost, in the context of a Reiki session, I wanted to protect every animal's dignity and also their right to empowerment because it's so important that they have a voice in the process of Reiki and that our human "good intentions" don't carry us away from the animal's own unique preferences and journey. You know we mean well—the reason we practice animal Reiki is because we want to help heal the animal—but so often our agenda takes over; it's our human need to do and to fix that causes this. As much as we mean well and as much as we love animals, we forget that they should lead this process, and we should empower them to do that. I believe that our process and approach has to protect and ensure their empowerment. It's also important that we always come from a place of receptivity and remember that animals are our teachers. Because so many times I see all over the internet, you know, "Animal healers"; in other words people who heal animals—"Look at these healers, they're healing animals; this animal had this problem, and this animal has that problem, and this person healed it!" For me this is such an egotistical way to look at the healing process instead of all the depth and beauty and "two-way" nature of what exactly is happening.

Viewing it from our human ego is not giving animals any credit for what they bring to the shared process of healing between practitioner and client, and thus we are not honoring the wisdom of animal healing. I want to protect animals' dignity and empower them in that way. Over the years, I learned that when I had the most successful Reiki treatments, it was through empowering animals to lead the way and through listening to their wisdom. I really wanted to honor that and help awaken others to this amazing possibility. And so that was one reason, probably the very most important reason, for the code.

2.   Another reason why I wrote a code of ethics was that I wanted to help animals by helping humans. Humans have to reach out to animals to help them, but what if Reiki and these ethics can help us reach out in the most helpful, most loving way—full of compassion so that animal suffering is eased? I want animal lovers to be the healing change they want to see in the world, and with Reiki that really starts with us, with each of our spirits. It ripples out to our own animal family and then we get inspired to go out and help other animals, maybe out

to a friend's animal, and then hopefully we get inspired to go out even further into the community and help animals outside our immediate circle. I wanted to create this code of ethics to help humans do that—to create a standard of approach and an ethical foundation so that humans could go out and help many animals in the community through Reiki.

The third reason that I wrote the code of ethics was to help bring together the Animal Reiki community. Many of us feel really isolated—not only from other holistic modalities that might use a very different approach than us but also from the veterinary community because they don't always understand the non-invasive approach that Reiki gives that can do no harm. And so this code of ethics helps all of us in the Animal Reiki community to hold hands together in unity for the good of all beings, regardless of species.

And that brings me to the fourth reason why I wrote this code of ethics. I wanted to clarify the differences between how we share Reiki with humans, and how we should not use a human approach when sharing Reiki with animals. In most Reiki circles, animals are at best, a footnote in Reiki courses. For example, you might go to a class and it's a Reiki 1 course and they'll spend the whole time talking about people working with self-treatment, people working with treatments and people, and using Reiki for everything else, and at the end they might say "Oh, also you can use it on animals, whatever... all living beings, okay, that's it, congratulations, you're done." So it's very much footnoted—I mean that's how I was taught, to be honest—because there weren't Animal Reiki books, specialty classes or e-courses per se when I started with Reiki back in the 90s.

Since that's exactly how I was taught, I started my whole practice based on all the rules I had learned for humans. But as I worked more with animals I would run into quite a few problems. As any of you who have taken my courses know, sometimes I tell those stories of how I ended up having to put a dog on a leash so he didn't leave so that I could do Reiki on him. Or I would cross-tie large animals so I could do Reiki on them. And it was just very hands on, touch-based, very much like the way, of course, that we work with people; some animals submitted to it and said, "Well, okay, fine," but a lot of animals didn't want anything to do with it, and so I found myself not feeling good about what was happening. That's what got me looking for a different road, or a different approach, for using Reiki techniques in a different way that would resonate with animals, and cause them to be drawn to me rather than repelled by me.

I think this code of ethics is simply clarifying these differences in approach and honoring them. Animals are not only our clients; they're also our teachers because, I believe, they are more spiritually evolved. I believe they can guide and inform our journey as Reiki practitioners and they deserve to be approached with a humble heart. They deserve to be allowed to be who they are, instead of having to be in a box of what we think they should act like, what we think they should do when we're "doing Reiki." I believe that in Animal Reiki, we need to meet them where they are and let go of pre-conceived notions instead of asking them to conform to our narrow human ideas of what it means to do Reiki.

5.   I wanted to highlight all of these differences in the code of ethics. I also wrote the code of ethics because I wanted to

validate those unique skills and the inner mental and spiritual cultivation that working with animals requires, because animals are so aware of our inner thoughts and emotional feelings. We have to leave our anger, our worries, our ego, and all other negativity at the door if we hope to inspire enough trust for them to want to share our space. And that's a really difficult thing; we are used to hiding things from each other as humans, right? Well some of us are better at hiding it than others, and some of us are better at sensing it than others. But really in general, animals are so much more sensitive to our state of mind and heart, and so you have to leave your ego at the door when you work with animals.

That requires real practice: spiritual practice, daily Reiki practice to help us to be in this space where we can be successful in connecting with animals. This code is about validating those healing virtues that we have to cultivate within ourselves in order to work with animals. It's very special.

I also wanted to create a common starting ground for all Reiki practitioners who want to work with animals, one that honors and protects animals' special sensitivities and gifts. We all might bring unique talent, skills, and training to an Animal Reiki session, but if we all start from the roots of this code of ethics, then the tree that grows from those roots in our animal practice will be healthy and strong. Even if our practice is unique to our own spirit, our own experience, our own lineage, and the way that it comes through to us to make Reiki our own, we will find that when we start with a code of ethics in our roots, all will be well regardless of those other personal differences. This is why I think it is really important to have that common starting ground.

Writing a code of ethics also helped to express the power of our practice of heart to heart healing with a language that gives credibility to our profession, a profession that asks us to take all the time and patience necessary to draw the human ego aside so we can truly listen to our animal friends and teachers. It's only then that we can be really present for animals with an open heart and a positive mind even in a difficult moment of their suffering. That might sound very simple, but in fact it's often very difficult and done only through practice, and so our profession is a very special one, because it is very powerful. Yes, it is very simple but only because it has the power to touch the essence of who we are. We are our hearts, we are not the bodies we live in—and the same goes for the animals. This heart to heart connection that Reiki cultivates is really, really special—to see it between humans is very beautiful but to feel that connection between species is, well, really there are no words to express how special it is, how powerful it is, how healing it is. Our profession is very, very dear to my heart and this code of ethics was meant to help give the profession of Animal Reiki more credibility.

I also want the information in this book to really support you to be more successful and for your practice, whatever it looks like, to really thrive. I believe that with the seeds that you already have, you can water and grow your beautiful practice with this code of ethics. I want to share with you why I believe that and where I was coming from when I was writing the code, so that you can see the purpose that each aspect of it points to. As we go through the lessons in this book, we will be touching upon different parts and different pieces, but they'll all come back to that original purpose of why it was written.

In general, I think that it's important to share that purpose with you so that by seeing where I'm coming from, which I think will resonate with you, you can feel safe and comfortable and good about not only really incorporating the code of ethics into your work with Reiki and animals, but also about incorporating it into your own inner practice. I feel that the code of ethics really came from my deepest heart, from a place of love and compassion, and so I hope you can really feel that as we go through the details in each of these lessons.

THE FOUR COMMITMENTS: KEYS TO A THRIVING AND ABUNDANT PRACTICE

What commitments to your Reiki practice should you make in order to have a thriving and abundant practice? As I wrote the Animal Reiki Practitioner Code of Ethics, I reflected very deeply on the heartfelt commitments not only that I have made, but also that the most successful and wonderful practitioners that I know have made to their Animal Reiki practice. If you can model your practice on the same four commitments, then your work with animals on a small private scale and, if you choose, also on a larger professional scale, will be a great success and will thrive.

COMMITMENT #1: TO PURSUE A HEALING PATH FOR OURSELVES AND FOR THE ANIMALS

Successfully thriving Animal Reiki practitioners are committed to personal growth and healing through Reiki. We know that the more committed we are to our own personal practice of Reiki the more effective we are when sharing Reiki with animals. So it's very important to incorporate Reiki into our daily lives, to really make it ours in our own authentic and unique way—to *be* Reiki every single day.

This experience of *being* Reiki is in essence the experience of the healing that happens in the space of oneness, of harmony, of unity. It's in this space, what I call *The Reiki Space*, that we realize we're not separate from animals. We can in fact commune and connect with them at the deepest level. And when we do this and we look at the world through our Reiki eyes, we can see the world and its animals with compassion, reverence, and gratitude. It's in this space that we find our heart's motivation to be truly committed to animal healing. Our daily practice really helps us open up our hearts in that way. The more we work on our own issues, setting a daily intention for healing, the more we become clearer and stronger in our ability to *be* Reiki with the animals—because they'll sense our pure intention to help them. They'll sense the energy that we are radiating. All that peace and humility and gratitude—they will be drawn to it. It's so amazing to see animals come forward and ask for a treatment, to ask to share our energetic space. It's actually a profound lesson in the wisdom of animals—their wisdom about energy, their wisdom about connection, their wisdom about how heart to heart connections create healing. Animals just know this, and we can see when they choose to connect and come forward even more clearly when we pursue our own healing path as a foundation.

COMMITMENT #2: TO SUPPORT
THE ANIMAL'S FAMILY

It's important to remember that when we work with animals it's not in isolation; we are also working hand in hand with their animal companions and also their human companions. When animals are sick or injured or otherwise suffering or in need of healing, both the animal and human family is affected. We can really facilitate our Reiki support by inviting family members, human and animal, to sit in the room with us during animal treatments so that all can be a part of the session and share and support each other. Sometimes as a result, the human companions might decide to set up their own separate appointments for their own treatment because when they're sitting with you and their animals fall asleep or they feel peaceful for this first time in a long time, they realize how good Reiki is and so they want their own treatment. Yay! Just because you're an Animal Reiki practitioner doesn't mean you can't work with people. In fact, people are animals—we've kind of forgotten it, but we are.

There's another reason to support the whole family, not just the animal client. By giving support to the family, you're compassionately validating the significance and difficulty of caring for an injured, ill, or transitioning animal. And you're also supporting and validating the importance of the role the animal plays in the family. This kind of validation is, unfortunately, frequently missing in our society. For example many people have shared with me that after their animal died and they went to work a couple of days later, and if they showed any kind of sadness or grief for more than a day, their co-work-ers started saying, "Well, it's only a dog" or "It's only a cat. Get over it." Others have shared with me that even though their animal was very sick with a really bad chronic illness or maybe their animal had a long hospice period, they had decided to care for their animals instead of choosing euthanasia. Often people around them would say, "Well, gosh, that's a lot of work and expense. Why don't you just put him down?"

This kind of insensitivity is all over our society, all over the world towards animals. So when you walk into the home and bring Reiki into the family, you're bringing healing, peace, and comfort, yes, but you are also bringing support through your acknowledgement and validation that this animal is very important to this family. This animal is an integral part of the family and that the grief, the worry, the sadness that everybody feels is okay. You are there to hold a beautiful space for that, which is, I think, very badly needed in our society.

If you find yourself working with an animal who is very ill, maybe approaching his or her transition, then you might walk into a home that is extremely troubled, extremely emotional, and everybody in the family might be dealing with this situation differently. It's important to recognize that your role as a Reiki practitioner is to just remain open and accepting of the feelings and needs of each family member. We have to stay centered and grounded, and that will help us stay peaceful and hold the space—that Reiki space—so that everybody can feel comfortable, be themselves and be open in their hearts for healing in that beautiful space that you're holding.

Part of what comes when we share Reiki with animals

is that sometimes as practitioners we might receive intuitive information about the animals, about their emotions or what they're feeling. Some people may receive whole messages. What I found is with Reiki, you don't need words. Reiki is beyond words, so very rarely maybe there is something that you receive intuitively that might be helpful to comfort people and that's fine to share with them. Maybe it'll bring comfort and clarity to them—that's great. But I really feel that the most power we possess as Reiki practitioners is in the quiet moments where the hearts of the practitioner, the animal, and the family are open and the communication of the hearts is so much deeper and more healing than communication of the mouth. So just close the mouth and open the heart: for me that is the best and most beautiful way to be—to be listeners, to be witnesses, and to be present for whatever comes.

It's also really important to let go of our own judgment, even in the midst of a difficult and emotional decision like the decision to euthanize, because that's really up to the animal's person and the veterinarian. I do always like to refer people to Gail Pope's books on the subject[1] so that they know and at least can educate themselves, about hospice and the potential for a natural dying process. Then comes just allowing—just making sure that they have all the informa-

---

1 Gail Pope along with her husband Richard Pope are the founders of BrightHaven Center for Animal Rescue, Hospice and Holistic Education based in Santa Rosa, California. Gail has written extensively about hospice for animals. For more information on this and BrightHaven's other services see www.brighthaven.org/about/

tion they need and then just sitting and holding the space, knowing that whatever decision they make is just perfect if it's made out of love. I think that is a really powerful and healing space that we can hold as Reiki practitioners.

COMMITMENT #3: TO SUPPORT OTHER ANIMAL HEALTH PROFESSIONALS AS THEY SUPPORT NEEDY ANIMALS IN THE COMMUNITY

I see every Animal Reiki practitioner as an ally to the veterinary profession. Now the veterinarians are the ones who are leading our community when it comes to health and well-being. So we have to create partnerships and cooperative relationships with other practitioners in the animal health field. This can often be difficult because Reiki is still relatively unknown in traditional veterinary professions, although more and more it is accepted in holistic veterinary offices, which is really wonderful. Also other animal health practitioners these days understand what Reiki for animals is all about—at least they have a small, beginning idea of what it is. It's really important to see ourselves not as the only savior of the animals, but to see ourselves as working in tandem with vets and other supportive professionals like animal chiropractors, animal acupuncture and acupressure people, massage therapists, trainers, animal communicators, groomers, pet sitters, dog walkers, and so on and so on and so on. All of these people are working toward the same goal as we are—happiness, wellness, and a good quality of life for our animal companions.

Every animal's path to balance and wholeness is unique.

It may require a combination of many healing modalities. So Reiki can be an integral and supportive component of any regimen chosen for the animal, because it always supports rebalancing and re-harmonizing wholeness. That's why building professional alliances by sharing knowledge with other practitioners and vets will bring new knowledge and insights to you as a professional. We can accomplish so much more together than apart. Seeing yourself as part of team is really important to be successful. And to further support the healing community, Reiki practitioners should reach out to animals that need it most—those in shelters, sanctuaries, and rescue centers. So many of us, because we are already animal lovers, might donate money to these organizations, some of us may donate time, but by adding the gift of Reiki we're simply stepping up to a new level of commitment. In donating our time and knowledge for Reiki treatments for animals or perhaps classes for staff and volunteers, we receive blessings and gifts that repay our efforts many times over. Many of Reiki's deepest lessons in animal healing are to be found within the walls of a neighborhood shelter, or tucked away behind the fence of a nearby animal sanctuary. And in addition, by becoming a valued volunteer for these organizations, we build community friendships that will last a lifetime.

COMMITMENT #4: OUR COMMITMENT TO EDUCATE OTHERS ABOUT ANIMAL REIKI

We are pioneers in the holistic animal health field, so we must learn to educate other people, whether they're other animal health professionals, veterinarians, or animal caretakers. We have to be able to talk about what we do with them. So, if right now I say to you, "Hey, you're an educator," does that make you uncomfortable? You want to work on getting more comfortable with that because we need to help some of these people understand the value of integrating Reiki into the animal healing programs that they offer. As much as we might like to just spend all of our time with the animals and not with the people, we have to educate the human companions of the animals with whom we work. Whether it's those humans that are living with them in their home or the staff or volunteers of a shelter or an animal organization, we are going to have to go through the people to get to the animals.

In order to do that, we have to create a language about what we do so that humans feel comfortable in letting us share Reiki with their fur kids. This includes explaining what to expect a session to look like, and maybe common, behavioral reactions to a Reiki session, like being relaxed, yawning, lying down—that kind of thing. And it also involves, and this is really, really important, it also involves letting them know that it is the animal, not the Reiki practitioner, who is in charge. The animal is in charge of how and indeed whether the treatment unfolds. So they can say no and they can say yes—then it's going to unfold exactly the way they want; it's not our agenda. We are following their guidance.

Sometimes it's hard to put Reiki into words, right? But luckily, the experience of the treatment can often speak even more powerfully than anything we can say, because animals are so wise and often show us so clearly what they want in their responses—not only that they are sharing Reiki and feeling that energy but also that they are benefitting; we can see the benefits with our own eyes. Animals are often the best Reiki teachers and the lessons they teach us are best learned when we are in a place of humility and respect because we know that the animals are active partners, and even more than that, wise guides for us.

If we look at ourselves as Animal Reiki practitioners within a larger Reiki world, since most Reiki practitioners train and work solely or primarily with humans, our human Reiki colleagues are often very interested in the differences in our approach and our methods when we work with animals. They can learn from us when we share the lessons animals have taught us. We can also learn from them—from their human treatment experiences. We can gain insight from each other, through talking about Reiki treatments in humans and animals, by looking into the depths of healing and what that process looks like—all the different levels for humans and animals through the universal language of energy, life lessons in courage, joy, hope, forgiveness, gratitude, and so on. These are lessons we can learn from each other as Reiki practitioners who work with animals speaking to Reiki practitioners who work with humans. And the more we can clearly and comfortably tell people about what we're doing, the more successful we're all going to be.

COMMIT YOURSELF

Try to set these four commitments into your heart—really set your intentions to uphold these commitments, for your practice, whatever it looks like—whether you want it to be small and personal and in your family, or whether you have big dreams for really changing the community where you live or the region where you live or even the world. Whatever your goals are, if you commit yourself to these four areas, you will succeed and you will thrive. Absolutely.

I hope that Lesson One of the Reiki Practitioner Code of Ethics will give you some food for thought. And that as you are ready, you will move on to the next lesson.

MEDITATION ON THE GUIDING PRINCIPLES OF THE ANIMAL REIKI PRACTITIONER CODE OF ETHICS

I have given all of my intentions and commitments in writing the code of ethics, and how all of these intentions and commitments are going to make you the most abundantly successful practitioner. Now we're going to meditate on the guiding principles. These principles are the foundation for the code of ethics. They underlie every other part of the ethics that we'll discuss throughout the rest of this book. So reading them is great but putting them into meditation so we can open our hearts and minds is even better.

We're going to start with some hara breathing. Your hara is the energy center below your belly button in the center of your physical being. You can imagine it as a beautiful sphere of light that grounds you, that centers you.

As you breathe, imagine on the inhale you can bring the breath as beautiful healing light in through the nose, filling your body all the way down to the hara to the lower belly. And on the out breath, expand that light out your skin into your aura and into the universe. And breathing in this beautiful light, filling your body, connecting to the hara... and breathing out, expanding this light all around you... And breathing in connecting to the hara... and breathing out, expanding. Take at least ten breaths like this: breathing in and connecting; breathing out and expanding. Then just relax your breath and feel yourself embraced in this beautiful space of light.

• For today only do not anger, do not worry, be humble, be honest, be compassionate.

Our first guiding principle is, "I believe the animals are equal partners in the healing process." Take a moment to think of animals who've been healing partners for you in your life. This can be in the Reiki context or just a healing context. Animals who've walked side by side with you, with love and loyalty, through good times and bad. Invite those animals into your mind and let the lesson they've taught you wash over your heart.

Guiding principle number two. "I honor the animals as being not only clients, but also my teachers in the journey of healing." Bring to mind animals who you've offered Reiki sessions to. What have they taught you about the importance of letting go of anger and worry? Of gratitude and compassion? Allow those lessons to flow over your heart.

Guiding principle number three. "I understand that all animals have physical, mental, emotional, and spiritual aspects to which Reiki can bring profound healing responses." Reflect on the beautifully complex nature of the animals you've known, perhaps an animal who has surprised you with her cleverness, her bravery, or her resilience. In truth, we can only scratch the surface of the wisdom and depth of our animals' hearts.

Guiding principle number four. "I believe bringing Reiki to the human-animal relationship is transformational to the human view of the animal kingdom." Think about your personal relationship with the animals in your life. The ones that live with you in your home, or the ones you've invited into your family. All those animals you've loved deeply and who have loved you deeply in return. Think about how these relationships deepen your empathy and compassion for other species and the wider animal issue, maybe in your community or around the world.

Guiding principle number five. "I dedicate myself to the virtues of humility, integrity, compassion, and gratitude in my Reiki practice." Remember to stay mindful of the Reiki Precepts in all of your Reiki work, formal and informal, private and professional.

For today only, do not anger, do not worry, be humble, *Reiki Precepts* be honest, be compassionate.

And breathing again into the hara, bring that light of healing in through your nose… filling your body all the way down to the hara… and breathing out, expanding the light out your skin, out into the universe. And breathing in, filling your body with healing light all the way to the hara… and breathing out, expanding this light all around you. And breathing in, filling your body with light connecting with the hara… and breathing out expanding. Take at least ten breaths like this.

Take a moment now to thank all the animals for being such wonderful teachers in your life and throughout your Reiki practice. Setting your intention to finish, take a nice, deep, cleansing breath and slowly come back…

THE IMPORTANCE OF SELF-PRACTICE

IN THIS SECOND lesson, we are going to discuss the ways to cultivate the wisdom of the heart and the ways to find and listen to your inner power, courage, and strength. The section of the Code of Ethics we will focus on is:

- In working on myself, I first follow the code practices by incorporating the guidance of the Five Reiki Precepts into my daily life and Reiki practice.

- I also commit myself to a daily practice of self-healing and spiritual development so that I can be a clear and strong channel for healing energy.

- I nurture a belief in the sacred nature of all beings and in the value and depth of being of the animal kind as our partners on this planet.

- I listen to the wisdom of my heart remembering that we are all one.

As we go through the lesson, I'm going to touch upon each of these different points.

Let's begin, first of all, by talking about this section of the ethics as a whole. In Lesson One, we talked a great deal about the inner commitments that we have and overall principles that we hold as Animal Reiki practitioners. Now we will go into a more in-depth look at this section of the code. This section is about working with self-practice. That's where we must begin—with ourselves. As Animal Reiki practitioners, sometimes we imagine that we begin with the animals, but actually with Reiki, we always begin with ourselves. That is the most important component. There are four self-practices that we're going to talk about in this chapter. Each is a way for you to create the strongest space for your heart to find its strength and wisdom, its courage, power, and healing. Your heart is really the center of your practice. When you come from a very balanced and healthy space with the animals, you come from that wisdom of the heart. That, again, starts with our own self-practice.

When we talk about our self-practice of Reiki, the place to begin is with the Five Reiki Precepts. How do we incorporate the precepts into our daily life and our Reiki practice? I want to start that conversation by sharing a meditation.

MEDITATION: THE REIKI PRECEPTS AND ANIMALS

For this meditation, if you can find a comfortable position to sit in… and if your animals are around you that's awesome! They can join in, and if not, you can just bring them to your heart and mind to share this beautiful space, or dedicate this practice to them. Make sure your spine is nice and straight. Your shoulders and arms are relaxed. Place your hands, palms up, on your lap. Relax your entire body as you breathe deeply a few times…

Now we're going to take ten breaths together and on each inhalation, feel the energy of the earth coming up from the earth into the base of your spine, and up into your heart. On each exhalation, imagine you can release any emotions, fears, and worries that you may have. Breathing in the strength of the earth to your heart, and breathing out… releasing fears, emotions, and worries. With each successive breath, feel more and more stillness and stability within you. Breathing in and breathing out at your own pace… Bringing that earth energy up, unifying with the earth, and breathing out with love and light. Any worries and fears can just be dissipated into the strength of the earth. The earth can easily hold everything with love. Breathing in the grounding and strength and breathing out… Breathing in and breathing out…

Feel how you're becoming calmer and more peaceful with each breath. When you reach your tenth breath, relax and just sit in that beautiful space of earth energy and stability. Feel how calm and balanced the space is. You're fully supported by the earth...

Now I'd like you to simply invite your animal to share the space with you. Set your intention and open your heart, and invite our animal to share this calm, grounded space...

Now let's recite the Five Reiki Precepts. For today only, do not anger... do not worry... be humble... be honest... be compassionate to yourself and others. Let's bring these precepts into our hearts... and our minds. Let's contemplate what they mean. In your life... how do your animals teach you to let go of anger and worries? How do they show you humility, honesty, and compassion?... Perhaps your animals model these qualities for you. They're a living embodiment of them... How can the precepts help you as a caretaker to your beloved animal? How can they help you to be truly present for them? If you let go of anger and worry, you can come from a place of humility and honesty. If you're compassionate with yourself and others, how does that help you to help your animal?... Allow your mind and heart to sit for a bit in contemplation...

Now I want you to take a moment to thank your animal for being a healing teacher in your life. Feel that gratitude and praise for both you and your animal... Let go of any expectations... no need to worry about what needs to be healed... Just relax into this beautiful space of gratitude. If you feel your mind wandering, go back to the breath. Breathing in earth energy into your heart... and allowing any worries or fears to release with love and light back into the earth... Remember to let go of the doing of healing. The most powerful healing you can offer right now in this moment is to bring all your awareness and be here. Now open your heart and just be...

For today only, do not anger... do not worry... be humble... be honest... be compassionate...

And now set your intention to finish, again giving gratitude to the animals for sharing the space with you; take a nice, deep, cleansing breath, and slowly come back...

FOCUS 1: IN WORKING ON MYSELF, I FIRST FOLLOW THE CODE PRACTICES BY INCORPORATING THE GUIDANCE OF THE FIVE REIKI PRECEPTS INTO MY DAILY LIFE AND REIKI PRACTICE.

As we contemplate the first point of incorporating the Five Reiki Precepts into our daily life and Reiki practice, I want to talk about something that I call a radiance of Reiki. This is the healing space that Reiki creates around us in every single moment that comes from our practice of Reiki, but even more centrally comes from the Reiki Precepts. The word "Reiki" we can translate as a spiritual energy. That points toward our inner self, our inner essence, of compassion. One of the misunderstandings of the way Reiki works is that we are somehow doing something to somebody else, manipulating energy, or interfering somehow in somebody else's journey and path. From a traditional viewpoint, Reiki is seen as a personal spiritual path to rediscover our own inner, self-healing power. When we learn how to do that for ourselves, it creates a certain radiance of healing around us from which others can benefit.

Animals as we know are so sensitive to our inner states. They know when we're angry. They know when we're worried. They know when we're stressed. We can't hide it from them. On the other hand, they can also sense when we're balanced, when we are peaceful, when we are compassionate and joyful. That positive balanced space is our true essence, our true inner self, and that's what Reiki techniques help us get back in touch with, so that we can then support our animals.

If we're trying to get back in touch with our true essence, we must ask who we are, so that we can create this healing space. I think we learn how to hide our true selves from way back when we're young. We build a lot of walls. We wear a lot of masks as human beings. This brings us back to the precepts. A lot of our walls and our masks that we wear are built from anger. They are made out of worries and fear. They are constructed by our ego, and are there when we aren't honest with our true self—when we're not compassionate with ourselves and others. The Reiki precepts help us to tear down these walls that separate us from our beautiful inner light—our beautiful essence that is always perfect, always healing, always strong.

It's interesting. I think it's so difficult to reconnect with our beautiful and powerful inner self because although we start out as children, very open, then we build these walls, and the older we get, the more difficult it becomes to reconnect, not only with ourselves, but with the world. Think about how connected we are technologically and yet in our own lives, so disconnected with who we are. We need to remember how to reconnect. We need to lower those walls so that we can open our hearts again. When we do that, we remember our inner true self, which is compassion. We remember our true purpose on this earth, which is to help others. Of course, our animals are guides for us—they help us to remember this—just as I spoke of in the meditation we just did with the Reiki Precepts. They either embody those precepts for us, or they inspire us to live in the precepts, so that we can help them. They are very wonderful guides for us.

So if we want to start rediscovering ourselves, we can look for help in the precepts. We can look for help in the companionship of our animals, and we can also look in that space of quiet—where we stop *doing*, and we remember how to *be*. That's really difficult to do in today's world—to just stop, be present and breathe deeply.

Do this for a moment with me. Let go of everything. Just close your eyes and let's take a few deep breaths. Just be here right now… Sit in the space right now, and breathe. Be with yourself physically, emotionally, spiritually, without judgment, and notice how you feel. Where are you in this moment?… Now, open your eyes. That wasn't so easy, was it? You probably felt some other thoughts coming in. Even in just that brief breathing exercise. Maybe you could also feel a little shift towards peacefulness with the help of the breath. That peacefulness is always there under the surface. We just have to stop once in a while to remember it. Our animals really help us to do that, because they are always present. When I'm standing in the pasture with my horse, it's very easy for me to be totally present in that moment with the sounds, the smells, all of my senses engaged and just being there, not thinking about anything else. That is a space where it becomes easier to uncover our true self inside.

Imagine if we could be our true self and be completely, fully present in every moment. Imagine how healing that would be. We'd remember that we're all One, that we're all connected. This would cause a beautiful overflowing of gratitude and compassion and healing. This awareness of the present moment connects us to so many other things. It connects us to our animals. It connects us to our own true self. It connects us to our purpose on earth, our beautiful purpose of helping others. This is the true healing power of Reiki.

Reiki helps us to uncover our beautiful light and radiate it outward to help others just as the sun nourishes the earth. There are so many beautiful meditation techniques in Reiki. All of them help us break through the walls that we've built, so we can connect and remember. Reiki also focuses on the mindfulness, where we train our awareness to come back to here and now. If we have an open heart and a peaceful mind, that creates a beautiful healing radiance that spreads around us; it starts within us then it spreads to everyone around us, especially our animals.

We need to practice the Five Reiki Precepts every day. The Reiki Precepts help us to come back to our center, to our true self. We have to practice that deep Reiki breathing every day. That helps us strengthen our ability to radiate compassion more constantly, so that these qualities then stay with us when we meet a crisis. Sometimes it's easy to say, "Oh yeah, I'm totally in the precepts, and feeling really great" because life is good. When something difficult happens, now how are we doing? If we have been practicing then it becomes easier to keep our balance, to keep our center, and not get knocked over and so scattered when we face a difficulty. That's why practicing every day is so important.

I see Reiki practice in two ways. I see it as a formal practice where we actually sit down or we stand with our animals or we walk with our dogs, and we actually do a Reiki focus practice, whether it's reciting the precepts and focusing on and contemplating them, whether it's doing heart breathing, or whether it is focusing on the symbols or chanting the mantras or whatever your Reiki practice is. That formal practice, I think, is really important.

I also see that practicing Reiki is also about using the Five Precepts, choosing a moment when it might not be very easy—for instance in a moment where you normally would react in anger and instead remember and focus on the precept, let go of anger. Or in a moment when you would normally go down spiraling into fear and worries, to instead focus on the precept do not worry and allow that fear to leave. When you would normally get caught up in being really hard on yourself, and instead, remember the Reiki Precepts and choose to be compassionate to yourself in that moment. Those tiny little choices in our daily life, these are also your Reiki self-practice. The more you do it, in those tiny little ways, the more it will strengthen the formal meditation that you do. In a bigger way, if you wanted to sit down with your cat for 30 minutes, that's great, but you also have

SELF PRACTICE

to do those small, in-the-moment practices all the time. That is what will really strengthen that beautiful light and the animals will see it, and they'll come to you. You'll be an animal magnet. They'll want to be with you. You will be radiating this peacefulness and put your animals at ease.

FOCUS 2: I ALSO COMMIT MYSELF TO A DAILY PRACTICE OF SELF-HEALING AND SPIRITUAL DEVELOPMENT SO THAT I CAN BE A CLEAR AND STRONG CHANNEL FOR HEALING ENERGY.

MEDITATION: THE
BREATH OF LIGHT

I want to do another little
practice called the Breath of
Light. In this practice, we bring
the light in, but it eventually
reminds us that we *are* the light.
In order to radiate compassion and the
peacefulness, I want you to sit comfortably again, relax your body, and follow
along here. Rest your hands on your lap, whatever feels
comfortable to you.

As you inhale, visualize your breath as a beautiful healing
light coming in through your nose, filling your body all the
way down to your lower belly. As you exhale, imagine you can
expand that light slowly out your skin and now into the space
around you and into the universe. Breathing in, bringing that
light through your nose all the way through your body to
your lower belly. Breathing out, expanding this light in front
of you, behind you, beneath you, above you… a beautiful
healing bubble all around you. Breathing in the light into the
hara, the lower belly, and breathing out the light, expanding… Breathing in, and breathing out… Breathing in, and
breathing out… Breathing in, and breathing out. Feeling
your edges soften a little bit into the light, becoming one with
that light. Now place your hands, palms together, in front
of your heart. Feel the peace radiating from you… Setting
your intention to finish, take a nice, deep, breath, and slowly
come back…

The breath is very important. The breath is the bridge between our physical self and our spirit. We can engage our minds and hearts with the Five Reiki Precepts and engage our physical body with this breath and our minds with this visualization. Then we become much stronger. Our light shines much more strongly, and it becomes easier for us to hold this light and its peace even in difficult situations. Remember that breathing is good for your physical body, not just your spiritual body. This is good for your spiritual body to help you remember that you are the light, you are the universe. But also, healthy breathing is good for your immune system, for your metabolism, for every single cell in your body. It seems so easy, but often we neglect it, because of our emotions. Think about when you get angry—how you breathe. Not healthy. Think about when you are worried—how your breath becomes. Not healthy. We can train our breath in the same way that we train our mind. This can help us to be a clear and strong healing force in the world.

Focus 3: I nurture a belief in the sacred nature of all beings and in the value and depth of animal kind as our partners on this planet

I want you to bring your practice into nature, into the world. That's going to help you to nurture that sacred space with all beings. Even if you are in a city, in an urban environment, and you see a lot of things that are not natural elements, you can still connect to your inner nature and to the inner heart of the beings who are around you. It's much easier to do if you're in nature of course, but you can even practice when you're sitting indoors. You can practice when you're standing outdoors. You can practice if you're standing in a park. You can also practice when you're walking. For this practice, just allow your senses to take in nature around you: Earth, wildlife, insects, plants, trees, and if you are in an urban environment with a lot of skyscrapers and there's not a lot of nature, look up at the sky, the clouds, and connect with all of that.

When you move, when you learn to walk as you meditate and stay mindful and breathe, you'll feel that your movement is supporting all of your body and sending healing through your arms and your legs, and that nature around you is also supporting you. If you are walking with your dog or with your horses, you'll notice that they will respond positively to the shift in your energy as well.

Another thing that I think is really important as a Reiki practitioner is to nurture this belief in the sacred nature of all beings—to think about your choices that you make in your life. Do you do this with compassion, and with kindness for yourself and others? Think about the choices that you make as a consumer, as somebody who eats a lot of different things, even if these choices are small little ones made towards compassion and made in a sacred way, whatever that would be for you. Think about becoming more mindful in all of your choices. Think about how those choices in your life impact animals, and impact other beings and impact nature. How can you have a softer footprint in your life?

These kinds of choices may seem small but will have a big impact in the world if we all start to make them. Little by little by little... That's something that I feel is also Reiki practice:

that we not only follow the precepts in our minds and hearts, but also make real-life choices that show compassion for other beings. I believe that thinking about and contemplating and making small steps towards compassion in every part of our lives is really important. That doesn't mean that we have to be judgmental towards ourselves. It doesn't mean we have to be judgmental to others. This is for ourselves in our own heart—it feels good and right to us to live more compassionately all the time.

A lot of what I've been talking about here is not just about "Oh, I did Reiki for 30 minutes. Now I'm ready to start doing something else." It's more about bringing the precepts into our lives including into all of the decisions that we make. If we really believe that animals are sacred, and that they deserve our compassion, then we have to look beyond just our meditation practice, and we have to look at our daily steps on the planet.

I love that Thich Nhat Hanh has a beautiful quote about kissing the earth, "Walk as if you're kissing the earth with your feet,"[2] because the earth is your mother. I've always thought that was so beautiful. If we walked every step with that kind of reverence, and if we made every choice in our lives with that kind of reverence, imagine how the world would heal. I think that part of the code of ethics for me is really about how we nurture this sacredness in our world, and that will look differently for everybody.

Remember, this is not coming from a place of judgment;

2 Thich Nhat Hanh, *Peace Is Every Step: The Path of Mindfulness in Everyday Life* (New York, NY: Bantam, 1992).

it's coming from a place of compassion and open-heartedness. If you can find that space within yourself and contemplate it then it will come naturally. You will find it easier to connect with the animals without judgment when you see through the eyes of compassion. We don't want to ever nurture judgment. We want to nurture compassion with ourselves and with others even as we work on creating a more compassionate and softer footprint in our lives with those around us and with our decisions. We can do that while seeing things with the eyes of compassion. Our Reiki self-practice really will help us stay in that state.

FOCUS 4: I LISTEN TO THE WISDOM OF MY HEART REMEMBERING THAT WE ARE ALL ONE.

This is what Reiki is teaching us as we look at the real essence of the system. It's not really about healing bumps and bruises and illnesses, although physical healing is often a wonderful by-product of the practice because it does create this healing space. What it's really about is reminding us that we're One with the universe—that we should live in harmony with the flow of the universe. That we should live in unison with our souls, with the earth, with all creatures, and that when we do, we have a naturally healing space. This flow is so quiet and yet has movement, and it's very changeable, but it's also very healing.

This universal flow is what we feel when we are truly connected in our meditation practice. When we're sitting, and we feel that peacefulness, that well-being that surrounds us in our Reiki practice when we meditate; that's the universe. The universe can flow through us more easily into our lives and into the lives of the animals we love when we do our practice. We have to, again, let go of our anger, our worry, let go of our ego, and open our hearts of compassion; the more that we do this in little choices, big choices, formal practice and informal practice, the more we will be able to hear that wisdom in the heart—that wisdom that is there when we get in touch with who we are. That Oneness and the wisdom speak very loudly.

Animals can also sense when we're approaching them from this open-hearted space. When we've let go of our ego, we're not thinking, "Oh, I'm a human, and you're the poor animal." We let go of our judgment. We're not saying, "Oh, you have this issue and that problem. I'm focusing on what's wrong with you." We have to try to let go of that. We let go of expectations, so we're not going there saying, "Okay, I've got 30 minutes. You've got to heal. Let's get on with the program here. Come on." We have to try to let go of this. They know that when we approach them by letting go of all these things that we're being truly present—that we're not asking anything of them—that we're truly *being*. When we do, they'll come to us and want to connect.

When they do choose to come forward, they will support us to go deeper in our meditation practice, and will support us to go deeper into our own healing, and we will, in turn, be able to support them when they need healing. We will access our own inner wisdom. We'll also be able to benefit from their wisdom. They will share their wisdom with us. We support each other, a beautiful circle of healing and support. We'll see it even with the severely traumatized animals, wild animals, abused animals, even ones that are shy or fearful—

that they will quickly gain trust in us, when we are in that open-hearted space where our wisdom is pouring through…

However, what often happens is that we think that if we want to share Reiki with an animal, we have to go do something to them. For example, we think we have to approach them and put our hands on them. We have an agenda, so we forget the wisdom of our heart. The Reiki Precepts are pointing us to this wisdom. When we sit with our breath, we remember that we are the light; we are the universe, and we have this wisdom inside. Very often, we forget it. We might instead approach them, and we've got an agenda, we have our ego, and we're saying, "Oh, you poor thing, you have all these problems. Thank goodness I'm here. I'm a healer. I'm gonna help you, poor little thing. Just stay there, I'm beaming some healing your way." We do this; we mean well, but we do it.

Animals are such great teachers. With that kind of approach, the typical response you're going to get is a wide-eyed look; sometimes I call it the stink eye. They look at us like we're crazy. They're going to want to leave as soon as possible if they can. They may only stay two minutes, if that. Or what if they are in a kennel, and basically they can't leave? Then we're going to see a lot of aggravation at our presence. Animals won't really tolerate connecting with us when we're in a space of ego. They are very honest judges of that. If we are in that space of judgment, they will not have any part of it.

The great thing about animals is that while we might be able to mislead a person, we can't do that with the animals. They'll help you to see when you're not quite in the right space even if you mean well. If you have a negative response from an animal, then you need to go back to the drawing board. You need to go back and check in with the precepts, go back to the breath, let everything flow away and allow your heart wisdom to come forth again.

I've had that happen in a Reiki treatment, where it may happen three, four, five times in a half an hour period of time. Where I get in that quiet peaceful space, free of judgments, but then I lose it. Then I have to go back and get it again, and then I lose it. Then I get it. The animal is coming and going. I'll be with you, no thanks, I'm leaving. Okay, I'll sit with you, no thanks, I'm leaving. And you know what, that's okay. Animals forgive us, but also it's good for us to see the relationship between our own state of mind and our emotional state and the animal's response. That'll encourage us to work harder in our Reiki practice, and work harder at creating that beautiful radiance of Reiki so that the animals will want to be with us.

Let's say you are going to a shelter. You know there's going to be a lot of traumatized animals in there. Take some time before you walk into that shelter. Ground yourself, connect with the earth. You can use some of the practices we have done in this lesson. Open your heart, feel your heart and your mind expanding as big as the sky, feel all that peacefulness. Get in touch with gratitude at that very moment. Get in touch with your sense of connectedness. Not the sense of, "Oh, I'm here to fix everything," but instead your sense of groundedness, connectedness, gratitude. Now you're ready to walk into the shelter.

When your energy is open, welcoming and gentle, it's relaxing, and animals will love it. You're ready to see the sheltered animals—you may sense they're afraid, suffering, stressed. Immediately, they're going to sense your calm and peaceful energy. They're going to step into that. They're going to start to change. They can't resist it. They love the compassion, the kindness, even the inner joy. We can all get in touch with that joy and goodness, even when we are suffering. That's what's so beautiful—that we can see animals who have come from tough situations shifting almost immediately into peacefulness, into calm, no matter how long they've been pacing and barking and stressed. A cat that's been hiding will come out. A dog who's been barking lays down to relax. We can see the shift almost immediately. Underneath everything, is your true self. That beautiful inner light, that beautiful heart wisdom is always there.

Just in the way that we build walls, animals also have walls sometimes because of abuse or trauma or illness or suffering. Reiki dissolves those walls and allows them to shine. We can see that transformation happen almost instantly sometimes with animals who are suffering. I love shelter animals, because it's so obvious to see the change with your eyes. But we can even see it in our own animals or animals that we love that have a very good life, but maybe they're suffering from an illness or have something. We can even see it in them.

We have to look deeper into the beautiful heart of the animal, the beautiful bright light that's shining all this potential for healing, and realize that is simply a reflection of the universe. That is the wisdom and healing power of your heart, and that is the wisdom and healing power of Reiki.

MEDITATION: RADIATING A HEART OF GRATITUDE WITH YOUR ANIMAL

Close your eyes, and have your spine nice and straight. Shoulders and arms relaxed... We're going to do some earth energy breathing. On the in-breath, feel the earth energy coming up into the base of your spine and up into your heart. On the out-breath, release emotions, fears, worries, thoughts... Breathing in strength of the earth and breathing out... With each breath, feel more stillness and stability within you. Breathing in the earth, and breathing out into the earth. Breathing in the earth, breathing out into the earth... Breathing in and breathing out till you feel grounded and strong...

Now I'd like you to bring an animal you'd like to share healing with to your mind and heart. See the animal here with you right now. Feel your connection... I'd like you to allow yourself to think about an experience you've had with your animal for which you're grateful. Just see that experience. Feel the gratitude welling up inside of you...

Now I'd like you to think about some part of your animal, of his unique being that's so special—what is that? What's special about your animal? Just allow the gratitude to well up again and flow out from you... Think about how wonderfully unique your animal is. What is this special quality your animal has?

As you are so full of gratitude for your animal, imagine now your heart can expand out of your body, creating this beautiful space of gratitude all around you... Feel yourself saying thank you, thank you, as you allow the animal to share the space with you. Imagine you can unify together within this beautiful space. All is perfect and balanced... Just breathing in the strength of the earth, and breathing out this beautiful space of gratitude... Feeling all the healing potential for you and your animal in this moment...

Now taking a moment to set your intention to finish and thank your animal, for all these beautiful blessings and for sharing the space with you. Take a nice, deep, cleansing breath, and slowly come back...

In this lesson, I've given you several simple, short meditations to do to help cultivate that inner wisdom of the heart or as I see it, Reiki wisdom. When we do that, we can listen to our intuition, and we can harness our inner power. We can find courage to bring more balance to decisions even in difficult situations. We can really change our world from the inside, looking out at how beautiful that is. That's really what the whole heart of the code of ethics is about—about starting with ourselves, and how that can radiate outward.

In the next lessons, we're going to talk about working with others—animals, people in groups and society, and so on. I wanted to really focus on ourselves first, because as you can see, it will shape everything else that we do. Everything we do with the animals starts with us. Everything we do with the animal people—when we work with the people who love the animals that we're with or if we're in a shelter with care-takers—the way that we work with them is really going to be dependent on this space we hold inside of ourselves. Moving out into creating partnerships with animal organizations or veterinarians or other people in the world is all going to be colored by this part, by our own spiritual practice for ourselves. That radiance of our heart energy is the foundation for all the things we'll cover in the next series of lessons.

Lesson Three
Working with Animals

As we move into Lesson Three, I am very excited about going deeper and deeper into this code with you. This lesson will focus on ways to cultivate the best responses from and connections with animals. The section of the Code of Ethics we will focus on is:

- In working on animals, I first <u>follow the guideline of working in partnership with the animal.</u>

- I also always <u>ask permission of the animal before beginning,</u> and <u>respect his or her decision to accept or refuse</u> any treatment. I <u>listen intuitively</u> and observe the animal's <u>body language</u> in determining the response.

- I allow each <u>animal to choose how to receive his or her treatment;</u> thus each treatment could be a combination of hands-on, short distance, and/or distant healing, depending on the animal's preference

- I let go of my expectations about how the treatment should progress and/or how the animal should behave during the treatment, and simply <u>trust Reiki.</u>

- I accept the results of the treatment without judgment and with gratitude toward Reiki and the animal's openness and participation in the process.

Let's begin our look into this section with a meditation from my *Everything Animal Reiki* book.[3] It's called, "The Bright Light Meditation." This meditation will help us set our intention and focus our minds in a very specific way. We're going to train our minds in a different way than we normally think about healing. It's very common to think, when something's wrong with our animal, "Let's focus on what's wrong and fix it."

With Reiki, there's a more meditative, open state of mind. We're going to learn how to go deeper than what's wrong to see the perfect light that exists within. This can help us to let go of the need to "do" and "fix," which, while useful in other times, is not the best state of mind for us to be in during our Reiki sessions with animals. I want you to practice this right now just for a few minutes, but you can also sit with this imagery for as long as you like.

THE BRIGHT LIGHT MEDITATION

Let's find a comfortable position to sit for this meditation. Relax your shoulders, relax your arms and your legs and close your eyes, then take a nice, deep, cleansing breath. Let it out

---

3 Kathleen Prasad, *Everything Animal Reiki: A Simple Guide to Meditating with Animals for Healing* (Scotts Valley, CA: CreateSpace Independent Publishing Platform, 2015), 54. For more information, visit www.animalreikisource.com/reiki-store/kathleens-books/

slowly. I'd like you to bring to mind an animal that you'd like to share healing with. See that animal here with you right now and feel your connection.

You might have in your mind all the qualities of your animal, the things you love about him or her. Maybe there's also a healing issue. I'd like you now to step back from your own understanding of the things that need healing. I want you to remember that you are already filled with the light and wisdom of the healing energy of the universe. Just visualize yourself shining brightly with this energy that radiates from your entire being, your whole body that's radiating from every cell this bright, shining, healing light and wisdom energy of the universe, and it's coming out of your physical body, and it's shining through your emotional and mental body. It's shining out into your spiritual body, so that every part of you radiates the compassion of the universe.

I want you to set your intention to support your animal in whatever way he wishes, so that all of your light, which is flowing, can support your animal to step into that light, step into that space to heal, and realize that your animal's healing journey is beyond your conscious understanding. Allow this beautiful, bright light to purify your mind, to release all worries, concerns and your need to fix or control a situation, and instead to shine, and feel all the worries and concerns just dissolving into the light, so that your mind can relax and expand, becoming peaceful and quiet.

Just allow the energy to flow, and glow, and radiate. When you feel ready, invite your animal to share that space; as you connect, simply relax your mind, and imagine you can radiate light from every part of your being. Take a few nice, deep breaths. As thoughts come up, just let them go, like clouds floating by. Relax your mind so that it's open like the sky, and just shine.

Now, take a moment to thank your animal for his or her openness in connecting with you in this beautiful Reiki space. When you're ready… setting your intention to finish, take a nice, deep, cleansing breath, and slowly come back…

I love this meditation because it's very simple, and also very powerful. It's something that you can do just for five minutes or you can actually sit with it for a full 30 to 60 minutes with your animal. We just remember to shine our light. That's it. It's very, very powerful not just because animals can sense and feel that light and step into it for help when they need support, but also because by shining our light, we are mirroring back to them their own perfect selves and their own inner essence, so that if they're going through something that's difficult, they can remember all of their inner power inside, which is very helpful for them to be able to heal themselves.

Remember in Lesson 1 when we did the very first meditation with the hara breathing, which is one of the most important Reiki meditations? This "Bright Light Meditation" is a kickoff to that in a way. It's a way to help you to relax and open your mind first, because as I said, we usually focus on the more narrow-minded thinking about what's wrong and what needs healing. When we're working with animals in the Reiki space, because they're so sensitive to our thoughts and worries, that's actually the opposite of what we want to do. It's hard to understand that—how can I help them if I don't focus on what's wrong? When we realize the vast wisdom and compassion of the universe, that there is such a flow of healing that is guided beyond our understanding and we learn to trust that, we can let go and not have to control things quite so much. We actually become more helpful to the animal by letting go of all of that control.

I think this Bright Light Meditation is a great thing to do before you connect with animals. For example, if you volunteer at a shelter, before you go into the shelter, sit in your car, do this Bright Light Meditation. Remember, you are the light; you're shining bright, and relax your mind. Then when you walk into the shelter, you're in a space where you'll be able to more clearly see the bright lights of the animals. You'll be able to radiate positivity and possibility, and hopefully not get knocked over so much by the stress and sadness that you may feel.

Let's move on to the section of the code of ethics that we're going to be working in this chapter. This section starts with the statement, "In working with the animals, I follow these guidelines." We're going to talk a lot about the different parts of working with animals. Of course, we started with the meditation, because we want to be in a really good state of mind and heart before we begin to connect with animals.

GUIDELINE 1: I WORK IN
PARTNERSHIP WITH THE ANIMAL.

What does that mean, to be a partner? It means that you have to work together. You have to listen to each other. You have to respond back and forth on a physical, emotional, and spiritual level. We're not just *doing* our session *to* the animal; we have to learn to listen. This is my favorite way to express it—this is about *being* Reiki *with* our animal, not *doing* Reiki *to* our animal. The key here is meditation.

How do we work in partnership with the animal? We must realize that Reiki with animals is meditating with the animals. But even before we approach the animal for our session, we want to center ourselves for a few minutes using a meditation. This is really helpful to get off on the right foot, so to speak. You can use the Bright Light Meditation or if you want, you can do the Breath of Light Meditation or you can choose another one of the Reiki meditations that is based on the Reiki Precepts or use whatever it is that helps you get really centered and balanced.

We are entering into this Reiki partnership in a way that is just like the way that shelter staff members strive to be when they are helping animals. One of the insights that I've heard from shelter staff is, "Well, what we try to do is we try to leave all of our baggage and emotional stuff at the door when we walk into the shelter." I think that's a really great philosophy, but it's not so easy to do. Focusing inward on a meditation practice can help keep your energy centered and balanced and your state of mind open and calm. These inner qualities are key in whether or not the animal chooses to connect heart to heart with you for healing. Also, Reiki meditation isn't just good for the animals; it's good for us, too. With animal caregivers—whether they're professional people like veterinarians or whether they're paid or volunteer members of a shelter staff—there's a very high rate of burnout and turnover. There's also a very high rate of compassion fatigue.[4] Practicing these meditations will also engage your compassion to take care of yourself in the face of these realities. It's good for everybody—for the animals and for us. Before we approach the animal, we're centering ourselves using the meditation. If you're working with animals throughout the day, this practice is something that you can keep bringing yourself back to.

Then when you're ready to do a formal Reiki session, you need to find a comfortable position to meditate in the presence of the animal. I like to suggest settling yourself maybe five to ten feet away from the animal. That's a good place to start, but at the same time, it depends on the comfort of the animal. If it's a feral cat, that might be too close. If it's a family animal like a family dog who wants to sit with you, then that's probably perfect. Even if it's a cat who usually sits on your lap, I would never go pick up the cat and put him or her on my lap for a Reiki session. We always want to start a little bit further away because we want to honor their choice and preference regarding physical contact.

When I say Reiki is meditating with your animals for healing, other people think, "How does that work? I have to sit down on the meditation bench, and I have to close my

4 My nonprofit organization, "Shelter Animal Reiki Association (SARA)," offers Reiki classes to so many shelter staff and volunteers around the world. I feel so excited—so happy and proud about this—because it really will make a difference in their ability to stay centered and balanced and in a perceptive place so they can be of more help to the animals. The animals can be supported even more deeply than they already are. For more information, see www.shelteranimalreikiassociation.org.

eyes?" Well, that's a more formal way of meditating, but I'm going to share with you three different ways to meditate. One is the formal meditation, but two of them are more informal and all of them are forms of meditation, because meditation is about your state of mind and your mind's focus, your open heart and your presence. Our openhearted compassionate presence is the space that meditation gets us to, and we can get to that space while we're sitting, standing, or walking. When we're with our animals, we don't want to go so inward in our focus that we are not good partners. Because remember, an Animal Reiki session is about partnership. For this type of meditation, if we're talking about sitting meditation, then you're going to be sitting still. You might be on the floor. You might be on a chair. It depends on the situation and your physical comfort. If you close your eyes, I recommend that you open them periodically in order to observe the animal's behavior and make sure that the animal is comfortable and perhaps even asking you to come closer. And if the animal has left the room, you want to be aware of that, too. You can also keep your eyes open with a relaxed gaze.

You might want to purchase a meditation bench because they can be more comfortable than just sitting on the floor.[5] If you have a certain sacred, quiet space in your home where you can go and sit with your animals that's great. You can make a little area where you put objects that are special to you to make it sacred, like photos of loved ones or statues or

5 I recommend www.meditationbench.com because they have a great selection.

crystals that have a special meaning to you; maybe a vase of flowers or a candle or incense or music.

When you sit down to do a formal meditation, all of these special items can help support you in going deeper into your inner space. Your animals in your home will probably find this to be their favorite space in the house as well and they'll want to come sit with you when you do this. This is a wonderful way to do a formal sitting meditation for your Animal Reiki practice. Or try to meditate when you're standing. Don't only sit in your special room that's all quiet. With animals, they're always teaching me—"Hey, Kathleen. Don't be so serious, lighten up!"

My horse, for example says, "Hey, Mom, I want you to come and meditate with me when I'm grazing in the pasture or when I'm in my stall eating my dinner." I'll stand with my horse and I'll connect deeply with the earth and I'll find myself connecting with all the natural elements around me, the trees and the flowers, the birds and the little critters, ladybugs, and all these little things around me. It's so peaceful—the beauty of nature and being present in this moment, when all I can hear is my horse chomping on the grass. It's the most healing, beautiful time for us to be together, and I often find myself smiling.

I know that whether I'm sitting at home or standing in the pasture, it's the same practice—it's about my mind focusing, and my open heart. With that reassurance, I feel comfortable keeping my eyes open out of safety. Even though my horse is usually very safe, you know horses can spook or they can accidentally step on your foot. You always want to stay aware. If you want to stand outside of the stall or outside the pasture, then you can close your eyes. Even then, remember to open them periodically to see how your horse or the particular animal you are working with is doing. Maybe you're working with a goat or a pig, a cow or chickens or geese or sheep. You can have your eyes open to watch how they're responding to your Reiki meditation. Maybe they're moving closer or farther away, maybe they're showing little signs of relaxation and connection. Maybe they just seem content with your presence. It's always such an honor to be accepted in an animal's space.

Being outdoors or even just having your eyes open at first may seem to make it a little harder to meditate, but you'll find that actually, being in nature makes it easier. I think you'll see that it makes up for any distraction of having your eyes open and that all the natural beauty will bring you back to your center. So standing meditation is a second great way to do your Reiki practice with animals.

The third is walking meditation. Actually, this is a very common practice for Buddhist monks. We give the same focus to our mind, the same practice, whether it is the Breath of Light or the Five Reiki Precepts meditation, or any other Reiki meditation that you are doing.

For a walking Reiki meditation, you can find a place to walk that's fairly quiet. You can focus on the nature around you. If you're walking your dog, you can imagine you're connected by your hearts not by the leash. You can also do this without your dog. If you don't have a dog, you can practice it in nature and just embrace everything around you, the trees and the flowers, the plants, the earth and the sky, the birds, and so on. If you're with your dog, then you can also notice your dog's presence in the moment, because dogs are very good teachers of how not to be living in the past or the future, but to be here right now.

This will help to bring you back too, doing this walking meditation with your dog. It's a little more difficult if you do it in a place where there are a lot of people, a lot of interruptions or your dog's greeting other dogs and you have to keep your mind on what's going on around you and be a little more interactive. But if you can find a quiet place where it's just you and your dog walking or just you walking, then even though at first it might feel like, "It's really hard for me to move my body and stay in the meditation," over time, it will get easier.

In the last lesson, I referred to a beautiful quote of Thich Nhat Hanh. He says, "Walk as if you are kissing the earth with your feet." That's because the earth is our mother. We're walking on our mother. So we walk with that kind of love and attentiveness and gentleness. I think that's such a beautiful way to walk when we do our Reiki meditation, to think of that appreciation for the ground under our feet.

All of those things work together with our meditation and help us to be in partnership with the animal, wherever they are. We're going where they are outdoors; we're not necessarily requiring them to be in our space unless they want to be. We have to learn to be more flexible in our meditation. That leads us back to the next part of the code of ethics.

GUIDELINE 2: I ALWAYS ASK PERMISSION OF THE ANIMAL BEFORE BEGINNING, AND RESPECT HIS OR HER DECISION TO ACCEPT OR REFUSE ANY TREATMENT. I LISTEN INTUITIVELY AND OBSERVE THE ANIMAL'S BODY LANGUAGE IN DETERMINING THE RESPONSE.

People often ask me questions about permission. We talk a lot about it in all three levels of my Reiki classes, so I think it's important to cover here as well. I like to use different words to describe what I mean by permission. Sometimes I actually ask the animal for permission, which means that I might say, "Would you like some Reiki today?" I might say it out loud, or I might say it in my heart when I greet the animal. If the animal seems comfortable with my presence, happy I'm there, that's a yes. If I sense indifference, or that the animal is not really paying attention to me, that means maybe. If the animal is really upset with my presence and not happy about it, then that might be a no. In the last case, I might give it a few minutes to see if the response really is a no, perhaps because there's an initial fear that I'm going to do something hurtful, as is the case with abused animals. When they first see a person walking toward them, they just freak out. I give animals like that a few minutes to settle down. When they feel the energy of the meditation and realize I'm not doing anything to them and I'm not asking anything of them and I'm not pushing anything on them, normally they'll really quiet down.

On my homepage,[6] I've put up a video of before and after treatments at The Devoted Barn.[7] There are feral dogs and severely traumatized and abused dogs being cared for at Devoted Barn and they do amazing things with these dogs. The video is a great example of the response that abused animals can have to people who share the gift of Reiki with them. You can see how on day one, the dogs were barking and really aggravated by our presence. It wasn't that they didn't want Reiki—it was that they were very fearful of who we were. When 14 strangers walked into their space, they got very nervous and afraid. It took us that first afternoon to convince them, "We're not here to hurt you." When we got deeper into our meditation, they were able to really see us as a beautiful bright light and not as human beings that they might associate with abuse or fear. It was really interesting to see how through meditation Reiki helped us soften our humanness in a way, giving us the ability to meet the dogs in a deeper heart to heart space. By asking permission, it's on the animal's terms and so there can be progress over time for abused animals; thinking about our openness of mind and not pushing anything on them is really key.

Sometimes, animals who we know were not abused do not want Reiki. I've been in the situation, years back, where a horse who I did Reiki with all the time and who was normally very open to it, on this particular day was clear: "I don't want Reiki today." I respected that and I walked away, and then I came back the next day and he said yes this time

6 www.AnimalReikiSource.com

7 www.thedevotedbarn.org/

as he usually did. Permission is about listening and being open at every opportunity to offer Reiki. When you clearly see that the animal does not want it, ask yourself why. Yes, you could show the animal through meditation that you're not threatening. But if the animal is aggravated or upset and just doesn't want to connect, she is withholding permission and you need to honor that. These kinds of nuanced experiences are ones that you'll have to work out. The more you practice, the more experience you have, the easier it will be to see what is a "yes," "maybe," or "no."

There is a message here. At The Devoted Barn on day two, we saw such an amazing change in the animals' behavior—I mean amazing—how the animals changed on day two, and how grateful they were for the Reiki. And even in the case of my longtime Reiki horse, he decided that Reiki was not fine one day but was fine the next day. So the message is "Don't give up." Respect an animal's decision if she says no, but hang in there—that animal may really want to connect but have a lot of stuff to work through to get there. That's why another word that I use when I talk about permission is the word offering. It's something you offer, and that means that they don't have to take it. You're offering a possibility of heart to heart connection, but they don't have to take it.

I also love thinking of permission in terms of sharing because that also brings us back to that idea of partnership. We share Reiki with them, but in my experience, I know that I'm probably going to receive even more healing than I can offer, because animals are so amazing in that way. Being respectful of what I can learn from the animal and receive is also important, so I love that word sharing.

Another way that I bring Reiki to animals is quite different from what I have described so far— it's a dedication. Sometimes when I set my intention at the beginning of a treatment, instead of saying, "Would you like Reiki today?" I will simply say, "I dedicate all the energy created by this meditation practice to these animals." Then I go inward to my meditation and just imagine I'm radiating this beautiful, healing light and it's completely up to the animals to take it or leave it.

The idea of dedicating your practice to whomever is in your presence is a great way for you to let go of expectations and worries about what the animals are doing or how they're responding, because you're just doing the Reiki practice. The rest is completely up to them.

So it's very important to talk about asking, offering, sharing, and dedicating Reiki to animals in our classes. As you can see, they are all a part of bringing Reiki in a gentle and honoring way to our animal friends (and to our human recipients as well). All of these "permission" approaches have one thing in common. This is really, really important. They all empower the animals that we work with versus forcing our own agenda on them even if we mean well, because the healing truly is up to the animals. They're going to heal themselves, because we can't do it for them. Reiki meditation will help us to mirror back to the animals their beautiful strong inner light so that they are empowered to heal.

When we go deeper into this state of mind of empowering the animals, we never know what amazing things might happen. I want to share with you this beautiful story from my book *Reiki for Dogs*.[8] This is a case history about a dog named "Kaci." It was written by Leah D'Ambrosio, the vice president of SARA. The challenge in this case study was that this was a shelter dog who was really depressed.

> Kaci's story began when she was brought to a shelter by a good Samaritan after being tied to a tree for six years. The shelter staff worked with her for several months. She was finally adopted but sadly returned a couple months later. After six more months in the shelter, Kaci began to crash, a phenomenon all too common in shelter dogs. She no longer wanted to eat, howled for hours after closing time, and became deeply depressed. Leah had just completed her volunteer training for special needs dogs and asked if she could work with Kaci.

> Leah remembers, "Our first meeting was difficult, as all Kaci wanted to do was climb in my lap. After a few minutes of me reassuring her I wouldn't leave and that I was going to offer Reiki, she laid calmly half on my lap and half on the floor. She was so needy, that she couldn't stand not to touch me. As the Reiki started flowing, her body relaxed and her breathing slowed down. Although she never closed

---

8 Kathleen Prasad, *Reiki for Dogs: Using Spiritual Energy to Heal and Vitalize Man's Best Friend*, (Berkeley, CA: Ulysses Press, 2012)159–161. For more information, see www.animalreikisource.com/reiki-store/kathleens-books/

her eyes, she ended the treatment more relaxed than I had seen her in a very long time.

"The second week, we started our session with her [lying] next to me and her paw laid gently on my open hand. We sat together in this beautiful Reiki space for 30 minutes or so. When a couple came by to look at the information on her door, Kaci glanced up but quickly closed her eyes and went back into her space. I felt the sadness and hopelessness flow out of her. She had been disappointed so many times by people. She had finally given up. As we sat there, I whispered to her that she had the power to pick the people she wanted and that she did not have to wait for someone to pick her. She kept her eyes closed and acted like she didn't hear me, so I stopped and kept the Reiki flowing. The couple finally left and Kaci and I both sighed.

"We had been sitting in the Reiki space for about 10 minutes since the couple had left when a staffer came in to tell us that Kaci was wanted up front by some potential adopters. I told them we were finished and whispered again to Kaci that she can choose her family. Off she went to the front of the shelter, and I went to log out and end my day. As I was leaving the shelter, I had to pass Kaci, her potential adopters, and a couple of shelter staff who were discussing her needs and requirements. I started walking to the side of them so I wouldn't interrupt, and Kaci suddenly jumped in front of me with a big doggy smile on her face and her tail wagging frantically. As clear as if someone had said it out loud, I heard, "I found them! I found my new family!" It was nothing short of a miracle.

"The next day I went to the shelter wishing I would not see her, and luckily my wish came true. I was told she was adopted by a lovely couple who had Akita experience and felt they had found the perfect dog in Kaci." [9]

What a beautiful lesson of how Reiki can help the true spirit of a dog come out so that it's easier for potential adopters to connect. I also love this story because it really supports the idea of empowering the animals. Through Reiki we empower them, and it begins with our asking for their permission. We can realize that there are many ways to empower animals, once we start practicing it in the context of Reiki!

Once we set our intention in this open and empowering way, then we focus inward on our meditation for 30 to 60 minutes. Within that time, we allow the animals to move freely within the space, again keeping our eyes open so we can respond to their needs. If they want to come forward, if they want to move away, it's completely up to them. If we see signs of peace, relaxation, and connection, then this indicates that the animal is receptive to Reiki.

---

9 Prasad, *Reiki for Dogs,* 159–161.

A Typical Reiki Session

What does a typical treatment look like? I like to describe it as movement and ritual versus stillness and state of mind. And this is a key difference when we offer Reiki to animals versus people. People usually need the ritual of movement and touch to help them connect with energy while animals prefer connecting from a deeper place, more of a mind to mind or heart to heart connection.

For example, if you visualize a human Reiki treatment, you can picture the client lying on a massage table, with the practitioner moving around the person using hand positions on or just off the body, but the overall dynamic is that the Reiki client is basically still, maybe even falling asleep, and the practitioner is moving and following a physical ritual. In an Animal Reiki treatment on the other hand, it's best for us as practitioners to sit or stand in the center of the space, remaining quiet, meditative, and just holding an open state of mind.

If we try to impose a physical ritual like we do with people, it can often disturb an animal's sensibilities, and so animal treatments are most successful when we can learn how to drop the ritual and just turn our focus inward. Then while we hold the space, the animal moves around us. Sometimes the animal will come forward; sometimes he wants hands-on contact, and so on. The animal is guiding the movement, not the practitioner. That's the key.

Animals will be our teachers because they sense the energy quite easily. For us on the other hand, it's more difficult, so we have to let them be in charge. Their deeper knowledge of energy guides us, the practitioners, and they often show us what to do or, as I like to say, how to *be* Reiki.

GUIDELINE 3: I ALLOW EACH ANIMAL TO CHOOSE HOW TO RECEIVE HIS OR HER TREATMENT; THUS, EACH TREATMENT COULD BE A COMBINATION OF HANDS ON, SHORT DISTANCE, AND/OR DISTANT HEALING, DEPENDING ON THE ANIMAL'S PREFERENCE.

My best advice for this part of the code of ethics is to let go of the hands. Animal Reiki is not about hands-on healing. It's about heart to heart connection. This is not easy, because we like to rely on our hands—we're human—but to be successful with animals, we have to let go of the need for physical contact because it's typically not the way animals want to relate to us in a Reiki session.

Now, besides that, I think if we focus too much on touch, it limits us, because Reiki is so much bigger. Reiki isn't just energy that comes out of your hands and goes into whatever part you're touching. Reiki is compassion. Reiki is love. Reiki is the wisdom and light of the universe. In many ways, our hands are incidental. Some animals like physical touch, some don't, but we can let them guide us. Just keep our minds open. The more open our minds the more accepting animals will be to the session.

If we focus our minds on negativity, that's also not good, and if we're focusing on touch, then we fall into a trap of negativity. We're trying to touch the parts that are injured or the parts that we think we need to fix. For example if they have an emotional issue or we feel that "they have a broken heart," we want to put our hands on their chest over their heart and so on. What's happening is we think, "Oh, I know what the animal needs. Now, I need to put my hands there. Now, I'm healing the animal's knee, because he has a knee problem" or "Oh, the animal has an ear infection" and you put your hands there. Now, we're imposing our own thoughts and our own agenda, and the animals aren't partners anymore, because we are determining what's happening. We're not listening anymore.

There have been so many times over the years when I thought that the animal needed one thing healed, but then something else was the origin of that issue and needed to be healed. It was totally beyond what my conscious understanding was. That leads me back to that first Bright Light Meditation we did at the beginning of this lesson. We've got to let go not only of our hands, but also of our conscious intellectual understanding, because Reiki is so much bigger than that.

So when you're being Reiki with animals, don't focus on your hands. Don't put your hands up hovering over the animal like a predator. Practice sitting with your hands resting face up or face down on your lap. If it's cold, put your hands in your pockets. If you're standing, hang your hands at your side. Then allow the animal to come to you, not the other way around. Animals will show you what kind of touch, if any, that they want. They'll even show you exactly where they want to be touched. Horses will often move exactly to the different areas and so it's actually quite fascinating if you let the animals show you—the ones that do like touch. They might even go through a whole series of areas, putting certain parts of their body into your hands, which is really so cool when that happens.

Guideline 4: I let go of my expectations about how the treatment should progress and/or how the animals should behave during the treatment, and simply trust Reiki.

This is really about developing patience and remembering that there's really no need to touch, that the power of presence and an open heart is the ultimate healing. Staying positive and open are the most important qualities that we can hold, and we can only really do that by letting go of any expectations.

There are a couple of stories that I want to share with you that illustrate why letting go of our expectations during Reiki treatments with animals offers so much more healing. One of them is about the power of presence and an open heart, which is really the ultimate healing. This is from *Everything Animal Reiki*.[10]

> There was a kitten one day in the shelter where I was volunteering. He had been poisoned. His mother had somehow ingested poison and then the babies had nursed, and so there were three kittens and the

10 Prasad, *Everything Animal Reiki*, 7.

mom. By the time I got there, two of the kittens and the mom had already died and there was this one kitten left, and he was in pretty bad shape. He was very listless and couldn't open his eyes. He couldn't stand up and was just lying there. The staff person said to me, "Well, we're not sure he's going to make it, but we want to give him a little time; can you sit and do Reiki?"

So I sat outside the little cage, and after several minutes, the kitten tried to open his eyes and tried to move his head, and he leaned forward, and I could see he saw, he knew. He could sense I was there because, of course, animals are much more sensitive than people, and he was asking for more healing. So I opened the cage door. I put my hands in. I cupped my hands around him and he leaned his little tiny head on the side of my hand, and he was tiny enough that I could easily fit him just within my hands (and I have very small hands). He was just a teeny, tiny little thing. He curled right up and leaned his little head against me and slept.

After about 45 minutes, he woke up. I moved my hands away. He opened his eyes and looked right at me with his very bright eyes, meowed a teeny, little meow, stretched, and went over and drank water. Amazing, and with just one treatment of 45 minutes! It was literally as if he had come back from the brink of death, with nothing except Reiki.

What is more powerful than being present with an open heart and compassion for another being? Isn't that the ultimate healing? And this is what we do as Animal Reiki practitioners!

This is a shining example of how Reiki touches our most inner heart and spreads out in a beautiful ripple effect, and this is why we see these kinds of physical healings, as with the kitten. It is so precious to see.

This next story is from my *Heart To Heart With Horses* book.[11] It's about a horse named Nikki, a special horse at BrightHaven who taught many students about positivity. Nikki was what I like to call a Reiki sponge. She loved Reiki so much that she would fall asleep almost immediately whenever any of us would go into the pasture to share Reiki. Nikki had severe arthritis and had difficulty moving around. The first response many students had when they saw her was, "Oh, the poor thing." However, after meditating with her, you couldn't help but smile. She was such a sweet spirit.

Although Nikki's body continued to weaken and eventually gave out, her heart was so gentle and open, that everyone who spent time with her could feel her peacefulness and love. Even in her passing, she brought healing gifts, beautiful gifts of peace and freedom to those around her. Richard Pope, co-founder of BrightHaven, remembered his last moments with Nikki. He says,

> I settled down comfortable in my vigil with arms wrapped slightly around Nikki's neck and my head resting gently thereon. We were at peace there together in a still, early morning cold air. It was then

---

11 Kathleen Prasad, *Heart to Heart with Horses: The Equine Lover's Guide to Reiki*, (San Rafael, CA: Animal Reiki Source, 2016), 69.

that I suddenly became aware of a single gray dove who had landed just a few feet away from Nikki's great head and was simply gazing right at us both.

Time passed and eventually the dove turned and gently flew westward toward the horizon while we watched with never a movement until she could be seen no more. Suddenly, Nikki leaned her great head back and around to stare deeply into my eyes for several moments. She then turned her head again in the direction of the dove. At which time, her legs began to gently run. She looked back intently at my face one more time, turned again, and left forever.

Reiki helps us when we must look deeper. Supporting the dying process of an animal we love is easier for us when we can be in touch with our heart and realize that our heart journey with others continues on even beyond the physical. How wonderful to be able to look back on our journey together not only as two physical beings but also as two spirits and know that love never dies. When we look beyond the surface, we can see that we're never truly separated from each other when we are connecting through our hearts.

GUIDELINE 5: I ACCEPT THE RESULTS OF THE TREATMENT WITHOUT JUDGMENT AND WITH GRATITUDE TOWARDS REIKI AND THE ANIMAL'S OPENNESS AND PARTICIPATION IN THE PROCESS.

To help us experience the true meaning of this guideline, we're going to practice a meditation.

THE WHITE
ROSE MEDITATION

I'd like you to take a moment
to relax and to breathe, and
bring to mind an animal you'd
like to share healing with.
See your animal here with you
right now, and feel your connection.
Breathing in and breathing out, just
relaxing. Now, I'd like you to imagine
your mind as a beautiful white rosebud with many petals
curled up, each one representing each different thought you
have about your animal and each of his or her health issues.
See that rosebud there in your mind.

Now, I'd like you to imagine that you can drop this rosebud from your mind down into your heart and allow all the
petals of the rosebud to relax and open into the most wise
and beautiful flower. As this white rose opens in your heart,
allow yourself to let go of all the judgments, worries, fears,
or the need to control or fix issues. Just let it all go. Imagine
a beautiful sphere of light that shines out from your being
surrounds the rose at your heart, and this light is so pure and
so bright that all worry, fear, or imbalance is instantly dissipated and dissolved.

I'd like you to chant the mantra "thank you" in your
mind as you visualize the light at your heart going out into
the universe. Thank you. Thank you. Thank you. Imagine
your animal's heart is also a beautiful rose with opening petals
shining out. Together, your two lights become one as you sit

in that beautiful bright and open space with your animal. If you feel thoughts coming up, distractions, worries, or fears, start again with the rosebud in your mind, drop it into your heart, and open the petals. Imagine that each thought can let go into the light as each petal opens. Notice how full your heart feels as your rose becomes more and more open, letting go of your thoughts and just sharing that beautiful heart space with your animal.

Take a moment now to thank your animal for connecting with you in your beautiful space, and, setting your intention to finish, take a nice, deep, cleansing breath, and slowly come back...

It's important to always finish every Animal Reiki session in this space of gratitude with the animal. Always, as you set your intention to finish, remember to thank the animal for her participation and connection; however the animal chooses to show that, is always perfect. Sometimes we want so much to help our animals when we see that they're worried or we see that they're suffering from illness or had a trauma in their past, and so it can be very difficult to let go of our anger and worry, and then find gratitude.

Through our daily Reiki practice, we can begin to create a beautiful space of healing. Remember that Reiki time with our animals is a time to stop doing and to start *being*. It's a time to open our hearts and be present with loving-kindness. The power of loving-kindness and being is extremely strong. There is no greater power than this kind of compassion. Don't underestimate the power of being with your animal to help her heal. Reiki starts with a shift in our own inner space and ripples out to others. In reality, Reiki is not a system about doing anything. It's a way of learning how to be in the world with our animals in both happy times and in difficult moments—a way of learning how to be balanced, peaceful, and full of love. If we breathe, nurture awareness, find gratitude, and radiate compassion, no trauma or illness is so deep that it cannot be healed by the power of love. This is the real Reiki space that heart to heart connection creates. Remember now, as we finish this lesson about being with our animal, that our greatest healing power in life is not in what we do to our animals, but in how we are when we are with them.

WORKING WITH HUMAN COMPANIONS

WE HAVE ARRIVED at Lesson Four, where we are going to discuss honoring the human-animal relationship and how we can foster professional, supportive, and healing communication with animal caregivers. The section of the Code of Ethics this lesson will focus on is:

- In working with the human companions of animals, I will first share information before the treatment about my healing philosophy, the Reiki healing system and what to expect in a typical treatment, as well as possible outcomes, including the possibility of healing reactions.

- I will also provide a clear policy ahead of time regarding fees, length of treatment, and cancellation policy, as well as "postponement" policy, should the animal not want the treatment that day.

- I will never diagnose. I will always refer clients to a licensed veterinarian when appropriate.

- I will honor the privacy of the animals and their human companions.

- I will share intuition received during Reiki treatments, with compassion and humility, for the purpose of supporting their understanding of the healing process.

- I will respect the human companion's right to choose the animal's healing journey, selecting the methods, both holistic and/or conventional that he or she deems most appropriate, with the support and advice of a trusted veterinarian.

Working with the people caring for the animals we see is such an essential topic, because I think that for many of us, it's the more difficult aspect of what we do. Working with the animals is a little bit more straightforward just because of who animals are, and how much they understand what Reiki is, and how much they can lead us and guide us. Our communication with other people and their understanding of what we do is not always that clearly set out.

When we're with the animals, our responsibility is really more about being receptive and open and listening. When we're with their people in homes, or if we're in a shelter or a sanctuary or a rescue situation where there are the staff and volunteers there that we're interacting with, there's a whole separate aspect to those relationships as far as the communication that we need to have, and also in honoring the relationship between the humans and the animals. No matter where we meet the animals and their people, honoring these relationships is really important. I think one of the best ways to do that is through really clear communication.

Code of Ethics Focus: "In working with the human companions of animals, I will...."

The first point I'm going to talk about in reference to these words is what information we need to share with the human companions before the treatment starts and how to explain what it is that we share in a Reiki session. So to begin, I will share my healing philosophy about the Reiki healing system, and what to expect in a typical treatment as well as possible outcomes, including the possibility of a healing reaction.

How you describe your healing philosophy with animal caregivers comes down to how you describe Reiki. I think one of the great ways to describe Reiki is as a meditation system for healing that promotes peace and stress relief so that the animals can heal themselves. So this puts it right out there, that we don't really see ourselves as healers; instead we're supporting the animals to heal themselves. Besides the importance of creating open communication with the caregivers before you connect with their animals, there is another valuable reason for explaining your healing philosophy as it pertains to Reiki. Sometimes when people call you to come work with their animals, they know about Reiki in a human context, and so they already have a preconceived notion of what the treatment's going to look like for their animal—that it's going to be just like it is for themselves—well, maybe minus the massage table! If you were called in to offer Reiki to a horse, and they expected a massage table, that would be strange.

I'm being silly, but you know what I mean. People are going to expect to see hand positions, a structured treatment as to "where we are heading," and they'll probably expect that the animal is lying down and completely still. I've had experiences where the animal is peacefully sleeping in her bed, and the person goes over and picks up her cat, brings her over, and plops her on my lap. Or if the horse lives in a pasture, the person will have brought the horse in and cross-tied him, and then they're standing nearby in expectation, waiting for me to "do my thing."

This is a great opportunity for us to educate people about the differences. We can say something like, "Well, have you ever gotten a Reiki treatment?" If they say yes, then you can ask them, "What was that like? What do you remember about it?" Then, you can use that as the opportunity to say, "Actually, the dynamic between the Reiki practitioner and the animal is nearly opposite when compared to the Reiki practitioner and the human." You can explain to them,

> When you're a human coming for a Reiki treat-ment, you lie down, and you're motionless, and the Reiki practitioner moves around you and does a series of prescribed hand positions on or off the body, but you just relax and are open in that recep-tive space. You don't have to think about anything and just relax. With the animals, it's very different because they are so sensitive, and they are actually better versed in the language of energy than we are. We as practitioners must go to the space of being

receptive. We also are the ones that are more still and allow the animals to move. They may move around us. They may move back and forth. It's almost the opposite dynamic of what you would see in a human Reiki treatment, because we're allowing the animals to lead.

Explaining this to the human caretaker, who lives with her animal who is maybe very old and fragile and she might be very worried about his or her health, immediately puts the animal's person at ease, because now she realizes, "Oh, my animal gets to lead the process." Then, she's not so worried that you're pushing something on her beloved companion.

The same thing goes for shelter animals if you're talking to, for example, the head of cat care at a local sanctuary or shelter. You explain that it's completely led by the animals— that you're holding a space for them and then they determine what that treatment will look like. You can explain that you don't necessarily need to touch the animals, that movement on the animal's part is completely normal, and that they completely lead and guide the session, so that you'll just focus on the meditation and on holding that really calm, peaceful space.

The other thing that I always share about my healing philosophy when I am speaking with the caregivers is the importance of the practitioner's state of mind. This is something that you would never normally talk about with a person coming in for a human Reiki treatment. I mean, you might, but most likely you might say, "Just set your intention to heal" or something like that and then you would just begin.

With animals, it's a much more sensitive space because animals are very aware of our thoughts and emotions, and so it's really important that we learn how to be in a very grounded space with very peaceful energy. If we are having emotional turmoil that day, we are going to leave that at the door before we walk in, as much as is possible, so that our state of mind is very open. Open state of mind means that you're creating a space versus focusing on what's wrong, which is very narrowing. If you imagine that your thoughts can be as wide as the sky, that's our ideal because if our thoughts get focused on what's wrong and trying to fix it, then it's very difficult to stay positive and balanced. We become very focused on the negative, and that will cause problems for the animals, as we talked about in the last lesson.

So, I will talk to the caregivers about the importance of that state of mind and the openness and letting go of my expectations and letting the animals lead when I offer them Reiki. I'll let them know that the entire session will be a type of meditation. This particular aspect of your philosophy is a really important one to share. You might also have a website that you can refer them to that has information on this. I do have a lot of information on my website so when people come to me for distant healing treatments, and I ask them what they know about Reiki, I can send them to a couple of pages on my website to read a few things. That helps them understand my philosophy versus their preconceptions. When we educate people about this, we can head off a lot of problems later on like miscommunication, people expecting something that we're not doing, and just general confusion about what it is that we are doing, and so on.

The next area that I might talk a little bit about before the session is Reiki as a healing system. I might describe a couple of the meditations we specifically use or I might share the Five Reiki Precepts and say that Reiki is about using meditation to create this compassionate space. Recently, during one of my monthly Animal Reiki Talk sessions,[12] we talked about Reiki as a mindfulness practice. Sometimes, referring to Reiki in this way can help people understand what we're doing, how sensitive the animals are to that space, and that it really helps them when they're having difficulty, when they're suffering or in pain or having stress of one kind or another—that they can step into that space we create with Reiki meditation and it really helps them.

When I talk about the Reiki healing system, I also talk about healing versus curing. A lot of times, people think, "Well, you're going to cure the physical problem, right?" Clearly, we want to say right off the bat that this isn't about curing. Yes, often we do see improvements in different areas with the animal, but we don't really know what's going to happen, except that we know that we are creating this space of peacefulness and compassion and stress relief, and that that's going to be really beneficial for the animal. Beyond that, we just have to allow the animals to take that support that we give them and heal themselves in whatever ways they are able. It is not under our control. This part of our understanding is very important to communicate right at the beginning to the caregivers.

I also often say that healing is not just about a physi-

---

12 www.animalreikisource.com/animal-reiki-talk/

cal response—that healing goes much deeper, and Reiki goes much deeper. So, when we talk about that, we can hopefully get rid of some of the false expectations or confusion that people have about Reiki and what you're doing with it—and also what you're not doing. I think it's better to have that conversation before you do the treatment versus after you do the treatment, because if you wait, then afterwards, they could get upset because they thought you were going to do this or that. It's much harder to explain after the fact. If the person doesn't know what to expect, maybe during the treatment he might ask, "What are you doing? Why aren't you touching him?" Lack of clarity on our part as practitioners can make it very difficult for the person to get something out of the treatment, because as I will touch on in a little bit, we also want to include the person in the healing. So it's important to get us all on the same page right from the start.

We also need to talk about what we as Animal Reiki practitioners expect in a typical treatment. We've already looked at one of these expectations: that is, your philosophy on physical contact. One of the phrases that I like to use with people is that because it's meditation-based, it's really about touching hearts, not hands. You can say again how it's the animal's choice, and if they do choose to come forward for it, that's really great, but it's not the touch that causes the healing. It's the heart space that heals, which is much more difficult for us humans to sense, but that animals really can and they benefit from it. You can tell people about movement during the session: seeing their animal walking around and being more relaxed about it—that there might be an ebb and flow in how they take in the Reiki—that waking up and going and drinking something and coming back, and so on, is really typical and normal.

Another important piece of information to share before the treatment begins is that the Reiki space for this treatment can also be shared. Other animals are welcome to participate and we're also going to invite the people who are part of this in as well at this point, letting them know that the Reiki space is big enough for everyone. I also let them know that typically during a treatment, we see stress relief and relaxation on some level, whatever that means for that animal. We set all that up for them so they know what to look for and in addition, right away we're helping them to understand what isn't going to happen.

I also let people know that the way that I practice is that Reiki time is quiet time, so we'll save all our discussion for later. That's really important to express because a lot of people like to talk about the animal, and they might like to talk through the whole treatment. It's more difficult to get that wonderful relaxation from the animal if there is a lot of talking, because typically when people talk about their animals, they're talking about what's wrong and all the health problems. That can actually be kind of upsetting for the animal.

Sometimes getting people to understand why I have quiet during my sessions with animals is very simple and sometimes it becomes a learning experience for the animal's caregiver. I remember years ago I was working with a horse. He'd been really stressed out, and so the woman wanted me to do Reiki with him. She was standing there with us, and as I started the treatment standing with the horse, the horse started to get really relaxed within the first five minutes, and then the owner starts with, "Well, did I tell you, I've got a new horse? So now I'm going to sell him" (she was referring to the horse that I was giving Reiki to!) "because he's just not the right horse for me. I think I found people that want to buy him probably next week, but my new horse, she's so great." She's talking about this in front of her horse, and her horse starts to go ballistic. He starts to left up his head really high. His eyes get really white. Then he starts to move agitatedly.

So, I had to stop the session briefly and take the woman aside. I said to her, "You know, I think that that conversation was really upsetting for him." She responded with, "What? He didn't know what I was talking about." I explained to her, "When I talk in front of an animal, I try to imagine that they're like a five-year-old human child, and what I wouldn't say in front of a five-year-old, I'm not going to say in front of my animal. If you can think of it as your little child listening to you, then you can be careful about what you say." As skeptical as she was of what I was saying, she couldn't deny that the horse was really agitated, so I sensed that it actually did make her stop and think.

Those kinds of disruptive things happened fairly often early on for me, so I realized pretty rapidly that we need to let people know that it's a quiet meditation time. I make sure to let them know before we begin that if they have questions now, they can ask them now but that if questions come up or if they want to talk about something during the session, I will be happy to speak with them once I bring us out of the meditation. Then I make sure to stay for a few minutes so we can talk and they can ask me their questions.

Talking about timing, when you set up your time period

for your treatment, you want to make sure that your caregiver client (and you!) understand that the appointment lasts for however long you have set aside and that it includes the time that you talk to the person before and/or after. You're not going to charge for an hour, and then go out there and spend two hours, because you're talking to the person, having a discussion, or anything else. Your appointment time is your appointment time. If it is an hour, then everything gets put into that 60 minutes, okay? This is an important way for you to value yourself, your time, the information you share and all that you are giving.

The other part about working with human companions of animals, and I mentioned this in the last lesson, is that it's really important to get the person involved. This is vital because the human companion's health is tied really closely to the animal's health. When our animals are sick, we are not doing well either. One of my students who's been a veterinarian for over 30 years said that very often, in fact more often than not, animals and their humans share the same health issues, even if it's something really rare and unusual. Isn't that amazing?

I think that animals are our mirrors and our guides, and the more that we can find ways to heal ourselves the better it is for their health, and vice versa. The more that we can help them, the better our health will be. That extends out to everybody in the family, really, which is why I always tell people, "The Reiki space is big enough for everybody. We don't have to exclude anybody." However, there is another important reason for sharing this space and getting the person involved, which is that sometimes it is the only way to get the animal to relax and open up to connecting. I've even been in situations where the animal is very sick and very old, but the animal's basically saying to me, "Hey. I'm fine. You've got to help my person."

When the animals know this about their person, I can just see it in their eyes. If I ignore the person, and just go right over to sit with the animal, the animal can be really clear about what's going on: "Well, this isn't happening for me, I'm not going to connect because I'm worried about my person. He's not getting help, and so I just can't relax." This actually happened several times before I finally realized what was going on, and then I started to get the person involved. As soon as I got the person to join in the Reiki space, the dynamic completely changed. The animal was totally enthusiastic and all over the Reiki treatment.

If the person is open, and hopefully he will be when you describe Reiki—how wonderful it is, how beneficial it is, and that everybody can benefit—hopefully, the person will like being a part of the treatment. I've found two ways to get people involved in the treatment. One is by leading them in a meditation or a chant. You can do something very simple with them, perhaps just the hara breathing meditation or another meditation. You would lead them for maybe the first five or so minutes in the meditation, and then just have them sit and observe for the rest of the session. You can do the rest of the session silently if you like, or continue to lead the meditation, with quiet space here and there, for the entire time.

Sometimes, I've led people in a chant, and we've chanted for the first five or 10 minutes of the treatment and then we've sat quietly. There was one occasion where I was doing a treatment at someone's house and the person did a lot of chanting for his Buddhist traditions. He loved chanting, so we chanted then we'd sit for a little bit and then chant more. We created the space by chanting together.

That's not typical. Usually, I do Reiki sessions in people's homes just quietly, but you never know. You have a lot of Reiki tools, so be really open. If there's one tool that just comes to your mind that seems appropriate, like chanting did to mine, and if the person's into it, why not pitch him a chant and see what happens!

The other way to get the person involved in this healing space you are creating for the animal is to begin with a chair treatment for the person. Remember, the animal can benefit from the second you create the space, so you are not taking anything away from that animal. You can do the chair treatment for the whole session or just for the first part, and then have the person sit and relax for the rest of the time. For example, you can set up a chair, and maybe the dog is already in the room with you. Let's say you're doing an hour treatment. You talk to the dog's person for about five minutes before the treatment, sharing just a few basic things about Reiki, what to expect and so on. Then, invite the person to join in with the chair treatment, and do maybe a 15-minute chair treatment. At that point, you can put the chair away and have the person sit on the couch, and then you can sit with the animal on the floor or wherever you are comfortable for the last maybe half-hour, leaving the last five minutes to process what has happened, maybe explain some of what you saw, how the person felt, and so on.

These kinds of thoughtful additions to your sessions

are so beneficial to everyone. I talked about sharing your information about your philosophy and everything ahead of time—it's all part of getting people involved, making sure that they're clear on what you're doing, and giving them time to ask questions—that it's all part of the session. Once they know that, that they're an equally important part of the session, they don't expect that "she's just going to go in, and shut her eyes and be silent, and then she's going to get up and leave, and that's the hour." Instead, the animals' people understand that the Reiki treatment is much more inclusive. They are included in it and if there's more than one animal, you all can be in the room, and you can hold this space for all of them.

Reiki is an infinitely healing space. There are no bounds. It's just about us having an open state of mind and being willing to be open to all of these kinds of possibilities! The more inflexible we are about what a Reiki treatment should look like and who should be allowed to be participate, and the more we resist talking to people and sharing information about what we're doing, the more difficult it will be for us to actually connect to the animal.

If you're in a shelter environment where the caregivers are staff and volunteers, a great time to give some treatments to the staff and the volunteers, so that they can all experience it, is when you first come and you're talking about what you're going to do with the animals. Then, later, when you're sitting and meditating in the shelter, they understand better what you're doing and will be more supportive.

If you're volunteering long-term at a local shelter or sanctuary, which I hope that you will do, then it's great to schedule a regular day, once a month, where you go in for three hours—or even two hours—whatever you can spare—and do maybe 15-minute chair sessions. Having people sign-up ahead of time if possible will add to their experience, knowing that they are coming in and getting 10 minutes or 15 minutes in that special Reiki space. It will really transform their day! They will also get to know you better, as they come to see you as an advocate for them (as people who advocate for the animals) and it will help you to get to know who they are by having a little more interaction with them, which you won't necessarily do while you're sitting and meditating in the aisles or the kennels.

I've given you examples of how what you say and do with the animals' caregivers before and during a session can expand the support that you offer the animals. When I introduced this section of our lesson, I also referred to talking to the animals' caregivers about possible outcomes, including the possibility of healing reactions, a possibility that will definitely affect the animals. I am also going to discuss healing shifts.

So what is a healing reaction? A healing reaction really is a temporary worsening of symptoms, as things get better, or get relived. Actually, it's not common, but if you're working on, for example, a dog who has kennel cough or a cat who has respiratory illness or something like these conditions, the animal might start sneezing or coughing during the treatment. For me, that is a good and clear sign that the animal is getting ready to let it go, and that she is healing. This is why it is referred to as a healing reaction.

These are two examples of the kinds of symptom-related situations that you might see, but they're typically followed quite quickly by a sense of peacefulness and calm. So to begin with an animal might be feeling really sick and be pacing and then suddenly have a sneezing attack. After that, she lies down and goes to sleep—totally calm and peaceful. Let's say that you are working with an animal who has asthma. Understanding the healing response, you can let the caregiver know ahead of time that his or her animal might wheeze a little bit or might sneeze or something and that's okay—it's actually good if that happens—and then often, the animal will calm down and may even fall asleep, breathing much more easily. Again, these kinds of healing reactions aren't likely to happen, but you can mention it ahead of time if you want.

As in the case of human Reiki treatments, where the client wants to know what to expect after a session, the animal's caregiver will also be curious about this. I tell them that peacefulness, calmness, and relaxation are typical responses during the treatment and that these responses can last afterwards, and I also ask them to look for something more: I ask people to look for what I call healing shifts. A healing shift is a change from how the animal was before the treatment. It can be on a physical, mental, or emotional level. It really depends on the animal. It could be something that you would expect to see, and it could be something completely unexpected. So I try not to be very specific… like if I'm treating a dog with arthritis, I try not to say, "Yeah, well, hope he's walking better tomorrow" because there've been situations where healing unfolds in a way that is not necessarily what I would have expected.

I had one cat that had been spraying on the curtains, and his people were really upset about it. I went over there and shared Reiki. Then, afterwards, when I followed up with them, they said, "Well, he still sprayed today, but the weird thing is that he slept all night. Lately he's been up all night meowing and really aggravated and really unhappy and keeping us awake. It's been really hard, but he slept through the whole night, thank goodness!" That was a big shift. That for me shows that he's shifting back into balance, and so hopefully everything else will start to get better too.

Those are the kind of things that I talk about as far as possible outcomes. And with that, we have covered all of the aspects of the first part of this section of the Code of Ethics.

Code of Ethics Focus: "Provide a clear policy ahead of time regarding fees, length of treatments, and cancellation policy, as well as 'postponement' policy, should the animal not want the treatment that day."

My suggestion for you is to offer 30- or 60-minute sessions. Offering the shorter session is helpful for a number of reasons: for people who either aren't yet sure about the Reiki or who don't have as much money to spend on it, or for people who are trying it out to see what their animal thinks or feels about it, or just for whatever reason they're not comfortable with the hour session—that it just feels too long for them and they don't want to commit to that.

I always try to give people a choice and let them go with whatever feels better, and then let them know that they can always change that. Typically, people who start with a 30-minute session may the next time go to a 60-minute session because they see that their animal didn't want the session to end. There've been occasions where if I didn't have anything going on right after, and we were at the 30-minute point, and the animal was just finally getting into it, I would say, "If you'd like, we can continue into the hour." Sometimes the person has said, "Oh, I wish we had more time." If I do, I'll say, "Yeah. I have time. Do you want to do another half-hour?" "Absolutely!"

Of course you can't always do that, because sometimes you have other appointments and you've got to be on your way. Again, I think it's really important to keep your appointment time within that session, so when you walk through the door, you have that introduction and expectation conversation, then you have the treatment, and you save a little bit of time at the end for questions, and give them whatever discussion that they want to have at the end. That should all be part of your 60-minute session. If you have that written up ahead of time for them to read, that's fine, or you can just say it to them. By the way, if you do have a form for this, you could add a short disclaimer that states something to the effect that "Reiki sessions are for the purpose of stress reduction. I do not diagnose. You should seek out your animal's veterinarian for whatever health concerns you have about your animal" and so on. I have an example of this kind of appointment and treatment expectations and disclaimer statement in my Level 2 manual for my students to use but you can just write something up if you choose to. We are going to go over the topic of diagnosis further on in this lesson.

Another area of information that you might like to add is a cancellation policy. I have a 24-hour cancellation policy. Of course, in emergency situations, I make exceptions. Remember the Reiki precept of being compassionate, right? But making use of the 24-hour cancellation policy is a really good thing to do if somebody forgets because you may have driven across town or to another city to have this session, and there's nobody there when you get there—you still have to charge them for that. I guarantee you that they won't forget from then on out. Just for honoring your own professionalism, I think that this is really important.

Next, I mentioned a postponement policy. What if the animal says "no" to the session when you get there? One of the things that I tell people in advance either through my cancellation policy sheet or our conversation is that this is really up to the animal and if the animal says no, then we can reschedule, but that most of the time, the animals say yes or they'll say, "Maybe. I'm checking this out." If as practitioners, we have that open state of mind—you know, everything we talked about in the last lesson about how to approach the animal—if we really keep all of those things in mind and in our actions, and then they're probably going to say yes at the first appointment and all the ongoing ones.

The animal's person may be wondering what a "no" looks like? How do we know the animal doesn't want a treatment? This is important to talk about as it relates to the ebb and flow of the treatment, versus a timid animal who's unsure of Reiki. First, I have found that no's are very unusual. Normally when I receive a no, it was my fault because I wasn't listening to the animal, or I came on too strong in my approach and I realized that too late. This is a great reminder that your approach will make all the difference. But occasionally I have worked with animals who, for whatever reason, aren't interested that day. So what that might look like is that the animal is aggravated at your presence, and it's clear that he wants you to leave. You can see that the animal is really upset at your presence, and as a result, won't calm down. It's not just that he is agitated in general, like a dog in a shelter, which would not necessarily be a "no"; it's like the agitation is directed at you specifically. You'll see it, pretty clearly, I think, if you're very sensitive—you'll see if an animal just is really unhappy with this. In this case I'll explain this to the person and always quit the session and come back another time.

In comparison, there is the ebb and flow of a treatment. An animal might be lying down, and you start the meditation, and he might get up and leave, and then come back for a little bit and rest and then walk away and come back. Walking out of a room doesn't mean that animals don't want Reiki. It might mean that they want more space between you and them. It might mean they want to go in the other room and curl up in their bed and relax, so I don't consider that ebb and flow of going and coming to be a no. I consider that to be the animal's right of empowerment, that she can choose where to be, whether that's moving around in the room or actually leaving the room. This is a positive part of an Animal Reiki treatment, and it can be good to mention it.

Sometimes a timid animal might stay under the bed the whole time and never come out. That also doesn't mean a no but instead could be a maybe, and maybe indicates "keep going" on your part. A true no is about that really aggravated state that I spoke about. The animal is absolutely not able to relax. That is the no. That's what you would look for where you want to stop and then come back and try another time.

CODE OF ETHICS FOCUS: "NEVER DIAGNOSE. ALWAYS REFER CLIENTS TO A LICENSED VETERINARIAN WHEN APPROPRIATE."

This is one of the most important ethical rules of all. No matter what we as practitioners may sense or feel during a session, we must never cross the line into medical diagnosis territory. I always make sure to refer clients to a licensed veterinarian when appropriate because obviously, if you've been asked to do Reiki for an animal, there is an issue with the animal. It's important to find out what the vet said about the issue. If you ask the person about the problem and he says, "I'm not sure," then you're going to say, "Okay. Well, what does the vet say?" If the answer to that is, "Well, I haven't seen a vet yet," then you need to encourage the person to do that. You need to keep turning the diagnosis questions back to the vet—"What does the vet say? Well, I think a vet would be able to help you with that." You can always bring that up and really encourage people to take their animal to their vet, telling them that that is not your purpose, and that you aren't going to address that aspect. It's important to make clear that Reiki is never a substitute for veterinary care.

Bringing in the topic of vets brings me to the topic of animal communication versus Reiki and why it's important to keep the two of them very distinct. Reiki is beyond words.

It's beyond speech. It's about unity and connection. A conversation, as one might expect in an animal communication session, means that there is a person and an animal going back and forth. We want to go deeper than that with Reiki. Keeping Reiki and communication as distinct and separate practices will also protect us from the idea of diagnosis, such as when people might ask us what's wrong and might expect us to ask the animal what's wrong. That gets a little bit fuzzy and makes veterinarians a little bit nervous.

Let me explain more about my view of how we take in and disclose information that we may receive from the animals that we work with through Reiki. I want to begin with a visualization of the Five Reiki Precepts and how they relate to this. If you can imagine with me: If it is our whole being that heals, all of our physical, emotional, and spiritual layers, and this healing is like a sphere of light, then on the outside would be the Reiki Precept to let go of anger. Then, inside of that would be letting go of worry, so taking in both our physical and emotional selves. Inside of that would be a layer of being humble, and a little bit deeper, being honest. In the very center of the core of our being, when we have worked through all of our anger, and our fear, and our ego, and learn to be honest with ourselves and authentic to who we are, then what we get to is the inner core of who we are, and that is our compassion.

Now, that leads us to the Reiki Precept that asks us to be compassionate to ourselves and to others. It is that deep core of being within our innermost place of compassion that is touched with Reiki. Our most important healing potential and self-healing power resides there within that space of compassion and love. When we share compassion with the spiritual essence of our own self by doing a self-treatment, or share it with another being, healing automatically manifests. The ripple effects can be seen in the mental, emotional, and physical layers of our being. This is why we so often see many beautiful healing shifts after practicing Reiki. Getting in touch with our innermost essence is very powerful.

With Reiki, we connect heart to heart and transcend the limits and boundaries of language. We even melt away the differences of species. In this open space, miracles of healing can happen. Forget words and trying to figure things out, and trying to quantify, and trying to fix all the things that are "wrong." That's not what Reiki's doing. We're going much deeper into this beautiful space of unity and oneness.

Code of Ethics Focus: "Honor the Privacy of the Animals and Their Human Companions."

People often see this part of the code just as, "Well, if the person shares something with me, obviously, I want to keep it in confidence." But it's not just that. It's also about the privacy of the animals, because sometimes when we're in the Reiki space, we may know something about the animals. They may share something with us. We may receive intuition or have a certain knowing about the animal. We don't necessarily always need to share that with the humans. In fact, the only time I share anything that I might receive intuitively during a treatment is if it's directly affecting the animal's health situation for a positive way. But otherwise, I won't share it.

I'll give you an example. I was working with a dog who had cancer. The person was clear, "I can't lose him. I can't lose him. He is everything to me. He can't die. I need him." There was a lot of angst. So, we all sat together. She actually had two dogs. The other dog was really stressed out by the whole situation with the person. When I was sitting with the dog who had cancer, I got this overwhelming feeling that the dog was so tired. He just was so tired, but he felt like he had to hang on for his person. I just had that knowing and inner feeling.

But I really felt that this was a very private sort of understanding and knowing, and that there was really no reason for me to say that to his person. So I just honored and thanked the dog for sharing that with me, but I didn't relate any of it to the woman. It would have made someone who was already feeling panicked only feel worse or maybe even guilty for holding onto the dog. So I just didn't say anything. I simply honored the privacy of the animal and what he had shared with love and compassion.

What happened afterwards was really interesting. After that treatment, I didn't hear from them for a few months. The next time I heard from them, the animal's caregiver was like a different person. She said, "It was so great after that Reiki treatment. He started feeling better. We've had all this extra time together, but now he's slowing down again. I realized that this isn't just about me, it's about him. I just told him, 'When you're ready to go, it's okay. I'll be all right.' I really feel like I wasn't doing that for him before. I wish that

I could've, but now I'm ready to really support him in whatever he needs. When he's ready to go, I support that."

That was just time and healing. They had extra time for her to come to terms and to be able to support his passing. I believe it was Reiki that helped make the space for that to happen, not my words. I didn't have to share that really deep feeling that the animal shared with me—nor had I wanted to because I knew that it just would've made the person feel bad anyway.

So sometimes, it's better to just hold that idea of privacy with whatever comes up; just hold it with love and compassion, and with gratitude. That's all. Then, you don't need to speak about all these things, because Reiki will in some way just take care of it.

This is not to say that there is never a time to share intuition received during a Reiki treatment in order to support a person's understanding of the healing process. To make that decision, it's important to think very carefully about it. "Is this really going to help the healing process? Do I need to say it for the healing process to be helped, or not?" If the answer is, "Well, I don't know if it's really going to help. There isn't much of a reason for me to share," then there's no reason to share it. As you saw in the story that I just related, Reiki can take care of these things for us. But if the answer to your heartfelt question is clearly "Yes, it will," then remember to share it with compassion and humility and to thank the animal for entrusting you with this message.

Many years ago I worked with a service-dog in-training. He wasn't doing well at all, and they were thinking of dropping him from the program. When I shared Reiki with him,

I got the strong feeling that he was so sensitive to noise—that living in the kennels with the other dogs barking was very overwhelming for him. After the Reiki session, I let his trainer know this. She brainstormed ways to make it less noisy for him: taking him out of the kennels to a quieter room before typically loud times in the day, cotton in the ears to muffle the sounds if he had to be around the noisy barking of others, etc. These small changes made all the difference, and the dog was able to graduate successfully as a service dog!

This is one of the only times I can remember in all my years of practice where my verbal feedback was essential. Most of the time, I find that less is more in the conversation department where Animal Reiki is concerned.

CODE OF ETHICS FOCUS: "RESPECT THE HUMAN COMPANION'S RIGHT TO CHOOSE THE ANIMAL'S HEALING JOURNEY, SELECTING THE METHODS, BOTH HOLISTIC AND/OR CONVENTIONAL THAT HE OR SHE DEEMS MOST APPROPRIATE, WITH THE SUPPORT AND ADVICE OF A TRUSTED VETERINARIAN."

Just support humans, and let them and their vet make their own decisions about what they're going to do. If they ask you, and people ask me all the time, I'll often refer them to animal care professionals that I trust, such as Gail Pope, for example. I might recommend people to Gail who are interested in hospice care for their animal.

However, when I go to someone's home and their

animal is getting close to transition, I never ever say, "Well, you really shouldn't euthanize. You need to find a different way. Here's a book about hospice." I don't want to go in there as an activist with my own agenda, but I think this is a difficult thing to remember. We mean well, but sometimes our ego takes over. Remember that each animal and person's journey together is unique and so beautiful, and there's so much love on both sides. But there's also healing and growing that happens, and we're all on different paths. As a Reiki practitioner, I want to hold this space to support their dance of life with each other, whatever it may look like.

Maybe the way they see it isn't the way I see it. Maybe they do more conventional medical practices and fewer holistic ones, and maybe Reiki's the last resort because they don't really believe in holistic care. Maybe it's not the way I would do things, but it's not about me. I'm just there to hold the space with love, with compassion, without expectation. Like the story I just shared about the woman who didn't want her animal to go and was so upset, and then how she came around in her own time—more often than not, I've seen that Reiki can really bring people those light bulb moments for what's best for their animal. The best thing I can do is hold that space really strongly so that they can find clarity and peace of heart and mind, because they're supported with love and compassion and without judgment.

Now it's time for the meditation that will support you as you work through and with the information of this lesson. This is an earth practice meditation, because while we're working with people, it's really important that we stay grounded and this is a great meditation to help us do that.

MEDITATION: LIGHT OF THE EARTH

I want you to find a comfortable position to sit. Place your hands over your lower belly, your hara. As you inhale, I'd like you to imagine your breath as a beautiful light flowing up from the earth, and up through your legs, into the base of your spine, and into your belly. As you exhale, feel the breath flowing from your lower belly, down to the base of your spine, down your legs and feet, and returning to the earth. Imagine this light can connect you to the core of the earth.

With each breath in, the light can go instantaneously from your breathing in from the core of the earth to the hara, and breathing out from the hara to the center of the earth. Breathing into the hara... and breathing out to the core of the earth. Breathing into your center... and breathing out to the earth's center.

With each breath, imagine the light grows brighter and brighter both at your hara, and in the core of the earth. Breathing in... and breathing out... the energy circulating back and forth. Feel your lower body becoming heavier and heavier, as if there's no separation between you and the earth's center. Breathing in... and breathing out...

Just relax your breath now and feel the energy, feel the energy in your hara as a bright, warm light. Feel your hands connected to the hara, and all of your being also connected to the hara. Imagine that your hara is no different from the core of the earth, the same beautiful light emanates. Feel the stability and strength of the earth within your own center.

Imagine now that this light at your hara and the light of the earth can expand, filling your whole body with beautiful light. Your inner light is the light of the earth. Feel every cell of your body radiating the stability of the earth. You are a mountain, grounded and strong. Even more, you are all mountains. In fact, you are the earth.

Bring your awareness to this present moment. Feel the strength of the earth rippling out your body, into your emotions, and into your spirit, making you stronger and stronger, just as the energy of the earth ripples out into space. The earth moves in space yet is stable and balanced within the universe. Your life may change, and yet you are stable like a mountain. You are balanced and strong.

I'd like you to bring to your mind an animal that you'd like to share healing with. See the animal here with you right now. Feel your connection. Very gently invite the animal into the space, for whatever the animal might need, not trying to do anything or pushing anything towards the animal. Just imagine you are the earth, and you are there, strong and stable for the animal in this present moment. Whatever this moment looks like, you are there for whatever this animal might need.

Let go of the need to do or to fix, and just be Reiki. Just be. Within this space, you can share strength, balance and harmony for as long as you like.

Take a moment now to thank your animal for connecting with you in this beautiful earth space. Setting your intention to finish, take a nice, deep, cleansing breath, and slowly come back...

We have gone over many, many aspects of the human-animal relationship that arise through our work as Animal Reiki practitioners. I hope that Lesson Four has given you new ideas to think about, especially in building a relationship with animal caregivers. It's difficult sometimes to let go of our need to fix every situation with words and opinions, but Animal Reiki is a time to let go of the words and radiate compassion. The more we practice our grounding, the easier this will become.

Lesson Five

Working in the Community

WE HAVE REACHED the final lesson in this book. In this lesson, I'm going to explain and illustrate the concepts found in this section of the code of ethics:

In working in the community, I hold the following goals:

- I model the values of partnership, compassion, humility, gentleness, and gratitude in my life and with the animals, teaching by example.

- I work to create professional alliances and cooperative relationships with other Reiki practitioners/ teachers, animal health-care providers, and animal welfare organizations in my community.

- I strive to educate my community in its understanding of the benefits of Reiki for animals.

- I continually educate myself to maintain and enhance my professional competence so that I uphold the integrity of the profession.

- I consider myself an ally to the veterinary and animal health community. I work to support their efforts in achieving animal wellness and balance. I honor other disciplines and their practitioners.

As in each of the preceding lessons, I will also offer a meditation that will help support you as you grow in your commitment to increasing the health and education of the community of animal caregivers. This last section of The Animal Reiki Practitioner Code of Ethics offers guidelines on how we can use what we know and have experienced from working with Reiki on ourselves and with animals to establish and maintain strong and healthy relationships with the larger community of animal caregivers.

In order to successfully create an expanding, healthy community, I've incorporated five goals into the Code of Ethics. Let me go through each point one by one and talk about some of the things to keep in mind if we're contemplating going deeper into a partnership with the members of this community.

GOAL ONE: "I MODEL THE VALUES OF PARTNERSHIP, COMPASSION, HUMILITY, GENTLENESS, AND GRATITUDE IN MY LIFE AND WITH THE ANIMALS, TEACHING BY EXAMPLE."

This goal is really about living in the space of the Reiki Precepts: for today only, do not anger, do not worry, be humble, be honest, be compassionate to yourself and others. It's not so easy to stay mindful of them especially in unusual or difficult situations, but our Reiki practice can help us to do that. It's one of the reasons why I have included meditations in these lessons for you; meditation can become the anchor that will help you stay in that space of mindfulness. If we can be mindful in a difficult situation and stop a moment before reacting and instead, for example, repeat the Reiki Precepts either aloud or in our mind, they can help us know how to thoughtfully respond to this situation or any situation.

Imagine that you can overlay the precepts onto every situation, interaction, or plan that you have—in a conversation, in a Reiki treatment, wherever—just overlay the precepts on it and you will know the best way to be. Doing this really gets us to the space where we remember that Reiki is not just about a 30-minute treatment that we do with an animal and then we're done with the treatment and Reiki goes out the window and we go on with the rest of our lives. It's really about *living* Reiki. When you *live* Reiki in your community, then it sticks with people. People see that you're different, people are drawn to you, animals are affected in a positive way by your presence, healing happens wherever you are and people begin to notice that.

Knowing that people and animals are drawn to you when you live Reiki is a wonderful thing, but learning how to live Reiki goes beyond that. You are building your personal reputation, which is really the foundation for your business. And even if you don't want a business per se and instead are volunteering at an animal rescue, your personal reputation is still very important—you want to be professional even if you're not charging money, not only for yourself but also because you are a representative of Animal Reiki out there in the world. Not many people may know what that is—

although that is changing more and more—but their view of you can have lasting implications for our profession and for what it means in society to do Animal Reiki or as I like to say, to *be* Reiki with our animals.

Overlaying the Reiki Precepts onto each situation in the community will give us a guide to follow as we learn how to *be* Reiki all the time. I've chosen a few quotes that I really like to inspire us to model all of these Reiki values in our community. Of course, we all know that to model something is much more powerful than to say it. In other words, our actions are much more powerful than our words. Sometimes we stumble over our words in trying to explain to people what Reiki is, but if our life and our actions are steady and true to the Reiki Precepts, the words are not as necessary because people will see what Reiki is in a much stronger way.

Here are some ways to model Reiki values. Number one is to make choices every day from a place of compassion—compassion for yourself and compassion for others, and especially as an Animal Reiki practitioner, compassion for the animals in your life. Think about the choices you make every day and how you can bring more compassion to them for the animals. The Dalai Lama says, "Compassion is the radicalism of our time." I think that's such a beautiful quote. It's so powerful. In seven simple words, it says that often, making the choice to be a compassionate person means living a life that may be going very strongly against the grain. But we can do it, we're strong enough, and we have the precepts to support us in that action.

Another way to model Reiki values is to make a deep commitment to service for the animals. C. S. Lewis wrote that a really humble man "will not be thinking about humility; he will not be thinking about himself at all." I love that because it really points us in the direction of the Reiki Precept to be humble—but what does it mean to be humble? For me, it's about taking the time to volunteer in my community for animals. You may end up being a regular volunteer and doing Reiki part of the time. That's great. Or if you're not volunteering right now, you're thinking about what you can do to be of service to animals because that will be a very strong way for you to *be* Reiki in your community.

A third way to model Reiki values is to extend to yourself the same kindness that you give to animals. I know that that is not always easy of course because it's much easier to be compassionate and kind to an adorable little animal than it is to ourselves. Why are we so hard on ourselves? We expect so much from ourselves. We don't give ourselves any slack. We don't give ourselves time to rest and we don't nurture ourselves because we're givers and we're always giving to everybody else. Yet if we are going to model our behavior on the precepts of Reiki, we need to learn how to extend to ourselves that same giving spirit that we extend to others. I found this beautiful quote of Sanober Khan that says, "Whatever you do, be gentle with yourself. You don't just live in this world or your home or your skin. You also live in someone's eyes." Wow! I just think that is so powerful. It really gives us a feeling of connectedness I think, and Reiki, of course, is all about the connection between us: the heart to heart connection, whether with our animals or with other humans. It also reminds us of the importance of our actions. We need to remember to *be* Reiki all the time!

Another way for you to model Reiki values is to remember that meditation is life and life is meditation. Some of you have probably been experimenting with meditating—maybe just sitting, or even lying down if, say, you've been recovering from surgery, or if it's difficult for you to sit for physical reasons. Or perhaps you've been meditating standing or walking. In other words experimenting with meditation in different moments of real life. These kinds of adjustments to your meditation practice really serve to overlay it onto your daily life as a way to just "be" even when you're "doing" things. As I picture in my mind some of you walking and being Reiki, I can't resist bringing back the beautiful words of Thich Nhat Hanh here, "Walk as if you're kissing the earth with your feet."

If we can walk like that every day, not only when we're "doing" Reiki but also just when we are in life's daily routines, it will bring a whole new level of humility, of gratitude, of gentleness, of healing to every step that we take.

Goal 2: "I work to create professional alliances and cooperative relationships with other Reiki practitioners/ teachers, animal healthcare providers, and animal welfare organizations in my community."

This goal reminds us to think about joining forces with others. When we share our gifts and others share their gifts and we put those gifts together to help each other, we create even greater benefits for animals. Our knowledge and resources are bigger and better when we pool them. In this space of humble clear-seeing, competition no longer matters.

These relationships that you bring to others in the community can change people's minds one way or another about Reiki—sharing what it is and what it does can open people's hearts to it. By being Reiki, you are helping to create lifelong benefits for people and their animals. If you enter into a relationship with someone and you really touch that person's life, that doesn't ever go away. These kinds of relationships really transform people and their animals for the better. The relationships that you create in your community with others can also address really critical problems that we have in our society right now, like compassion fatigue and stress in people and animals, as well the fact that a lot of people are coping with challenging emotions like anger and grief. A lot of people are suffering, whether it's physical or emotional suffering, and we know that Reiki can bring relief. By joining together with others, you can do all of these wonderful things but do it in an even stronger way than when you're working by yourself.

Try to be receptive to collaboration and think about something called co-creation. I don't know if you've heard that term before. It's about creating something new together rather than simply thinking of things in terms of a simple exchange—oh I'll do Reiki and in return, you can do your thing. Instead, think of collaborating on something bigger and deeper. Remember though that professional alliances and cooperative relationships all begin with the personal relationship that develops, and that takes time. The personal relationship is the glue that will hold everything else together. So, you need to allow that relationship to grow organically; you need to allow the trust between you and the other to grow organically over time. You cannot rush it. In fact, sometimes when you try to rush it and you're too pushy, it can destroy a new relationship.

What qualities do we need to nurture as we grow these new and potentially productive relationships? We can find them in what we have learned through our Animal Reiki process. We can now let them come forward and serve us as we build alliances in the community. Number one is patience—being very, very patient. Number two is being really flexible and number three is being very persistent. These are some of the qualities that we've learned from the animals. Let's bring them to bear now when we're with each other as humans.

Let's say that you want to create an alliance or a partnership with a practitioner of another modality. Think about what you could do. You could give public talks or classes with other holistic animal therapists by working together beforehand to find a common topic and share about it. I have an audio course on my website called "Affirmations and Chakra Healing for Animals." I co-taught that class with an animal communicator. We each had our own perspectives and brought our own thoughts and ideas to the class, and that willingness to allow each other that space, coupled with the fact that we both shared a real love for animals and a desire to help people to help animals, made our course a really well-received success—for our students as well as for us. It was really a fun thing to do. Over the years, I've also done a lot of collaborations with my friend and colleague Leah D'Ambrosio, Vice-President of SARA, and those experiences have also been really fun. I've even done some with Frans Stiene, my teacher, which was really an honor for me and also, of course, fun. These partnership relationships have given me a clearer understanding of what it means to be a co-creator.

When we come together and we create something new, it's a wonderful way to expand and spread the knowledge and the healing. Again, it has to come from that personal relationship that's built on trust and service and all those other good things. You might want to think about supporting your local veterinarian. One of the first things that you can do to support vets in general is to always recommend to the human caregivers you're working that they get advice from their vets. I always try to bring this in to every conversation so that people keep thinking of them as their primary resource and that I'm more of a support to that. If you can, have a vet that you recommend and know personally, and that way you can keep sending and bringing more people to that vet, which is wonderful. It's a great way to let them know how much you support them.

There are many ways to build deeper relationships with your local vets. Offer free Reiki for animals after surgery as they are coming out of the anesthesia. Or offer free chair treatments for the staff (and to the vets!), maybe once a month or so. Offering these services is a great way to keep Reiki in their minds—in addition to recommending people and sending people to them, you're actually there in the office, directly helping their staff and the animals. They get to see how you work, they get to feel Reiki for themselves, and it's a great way to build a relationship. Over time, hopefully these vets might let you leave cards in their office; even more, they might try to recommend you to some of their patients; and even better, they might eventually let you use their office for Reiki treatments. I've had students do this in the past. From their experience, I can tell you that you do need to compensate the vets for the use of their office. Normally you would pay an agreed-upon percentage of whatever you charge the client or sometimes the clients pay the vets and then they'll pay you a percentage. Although this relationship involves some volunteering and then the fact that if you do get paid, you're earning only a certain percentage of what you would on your own, it's so worth it because the recommendation of a vet is invaluable for your growing reputation, which can give you the opportunity to be able to expand your therapeutic and educational outreach and help more animals.

GOAL THREE: "I STRIVE TO EDUCATE MY COMMUNITY IN ITS UNDERSTANDING OF THE BENEFITS OF REIKI FOR ANIMALS."

Look for opportunities to educate others. We've already talked about collaborating with another person, a holistic animal person or somebody who is known in the community. You can also educate others on your own, even if it's talking to just one person at a time. Maybe you're at a dog park and you meet a dog walker and you start talking to her. That can be a wonderful way too. Who knows who that person knows! When you talk about it, word gets out. You can also think about speaking to small groups, for example at the shelter where you volunteer. Maybe you could give a short talk for the volunteers there, the people that know you, or the entire staff.

You can also think about doing public talks or special events during your local shelter's fundraising day or at a dog parade or something else animal related where everybody comes out to participate. If it's a fundraiser for the shelter, you could have a booth where you offer people chair treatments. You could have some information to hand out and some pictures of animals receiving Reiki and talk to people one on one about what's going on. If your shelter folks or your veterinarian and her staff are really interested in what you are doing, they might allow you to schedule a talk to the public, an evening at their location that they will promote through their mailing list. You could have a small donation request of $10 to come to the talk, letting people know that their $10 will all be donated to the veterinarian or to the shelter.

These are all ways to get yourself out there to educate your community about the benefits of Animal Reiki. Beyond these there is the media. You can think about media like local newspapers and magazines—maybe have local TV reporters who do community stories about interesting things happening in the community come and interview you at the shelter. Also, think about social media. If you're not on Facebook or Twitter, it's something that you might want to think about doing. And if you like to write, consider starting a blog, where you can share your Animal Reiki experiences with your online audience!

Goal Four: "I continually educate myself to maintain and enhance my professional competence so that I uphold the integrity of the profession."

This is really, really important for all of us as Animal Reiki practitioners because while our numbers are growing, there are still so few of us. For example, in comparison to "Reiki with people" practitioners, we're just a drop in the bucket! So, we really need to work hard to keep and uphold our professionalism. We do that by continually learning and growing, by taking lessons in areas that improve and inform our Reiki practice. For example, I've taken over 500 hours of professional Reiki training. But it doesn't have to only be Reiki classes. It could be other areas that are of interest and that deepen some aspects of our Animal Reiki practice. Consider a complementary modality, taking classes on holistic topics like flower essences or essential oils or animal hospice courses. By the way, BrightHaven has a great online animal hospice course, which Gail Pope teaches. I highly recommend it if you haven't already taken it. Even courses like animal nutrition are important because nutrition is part of healing and the more we can inform ourselves about that aspect, the more it will support what we're doing with Reiki.

One of the students who has taken animal training courses with me now works with really difficult shelter dogs, the ones who have displayed aggressive behavior and because of that most people aren't allowed to work with them. By taking extra dog training classes, my student has not only gotten a lot of really good life skills in dog training but can now give Reiki to the dogs that nobody else is allowed to see. It's really cool that she's been able to help these dogs in this way, because it is quite possible that sharing the Reiki space with my student will calm these dogs and give them a chance to be adopted one day.

If you have other interests in connection to animals, think about what they are—what kinds of animals and what classes would deepen your understanding of working with those animals. Whether it's about behavior or nutrition or holistic practices, can you see that the more that we educate ourselves, the more we learn, and so the better we can be at our Reiki practice?

Now let's switch the focus onto other areas of continuing education. I also want you to think about education outside the animal realm—about furthering your education in the area of your business. I'm talking about marketing classes, computer skills classes, social media literacy, with outlets such as Facebook and Twitter, as well as writing classes. You could take a class on how to write about an experience you've had or how to tell your own story. That could turn into a Reiki book that could inform and inspire people about something that they didn't already know about. There are so many online courses these days that are available, so keep your eyes open and look for ones that can help you improve yourself by always learning, always growing and stretching yourself. It will also give you courage so that you can do even more, and you find yourself saying, "Wow! I never thought I could learn to use Facebook," or "I never thought I could work with feral cats, but I took that course and look at me now."

All of these classes are going to give you more confidence in yourself and in your knowledge so that when you're sitting with somebody's animals, you'll know that you have all these other skills that are helping these animals. Your vibration will just radiate that confidence so that you don't think, "Oh dear, I'm too shy to do this" or "I'm such an introvert" or "I don't know if I can handle this difficult situation." In fact, it will be quite the opposite because the more that we're learning and growing, the better we can be when we're being Reiki. This ongoing educational commitment along with our daily meditation practice ensures that we will be doing this growing from the outside in and the inside out.

GOAL FIVE: "I CONSIDER MYSELF AN ALLY TO THE VETERINARY AND ANIMAL HEALTH COMMUNITY. I WORK TO SUPPORT THEIR EFFORTS IN ACHIEVING ANIMAL WELLNESS AND BALANCE. I HONOR OTHER DISCIPLINES AND THEIR PRACTITIONERS."

I want to emphasize something I said earlier, which is that there's no such thing as competition. We are all here to support each other, to be inspired by the success of others, to allow these actions to help us grow and improve. Surround yourself with people who you strive to be like, who motivate you, who encourage you to move beyond your comfort zone, because these people will inspire you to be the best version of yourself. You know what they always say—you can learn a lot about yourself by looking at the people closest to you. So, if you look around at the people closest to you and you're not really seeing what you like, then move beyond your comfort zone and go out and make connections with a community that inspires you, that helps you to really grow and heal and be your best self.

Find a group that shares your dream, whatever your dream is, to help animals in whatever way possible. I founded SARA for that very purpose, for my own dream of expanding my relationship with the animals and to help others do the same. When you join a community or a group that shares your heart's purpose, you will feel supported in faith and love, and you will be able to do so much more with that support.

Remember that you are a unique, beautiful light in this world and your Reiki practice will help you to shine more brightly so that you can help more animals and their people. No one is quite like you. Believe in yourself. The animals need you.

Honor your foundation. Think about the animals and people who have gotten you this far. Hold them in a space of gratitude.

Be yourself. Create your own unique journey based on your most inner, true, and authentic self. Reiki meditation is going to help clarify that for you so that you can follow your heart. Listen to your intuition and your inner guidance. Regular Reiki meditation will help make this inner voice stronger so that it's easier for you to hear it and follow it.

Finally, let your struggles in this life, your difficulties, your losses and sadnesses, let them be your teachers. They make you strong, they make you unique, they make you you.

You know what else they do? They deepen your compassion for others and they develop your best qualities: your resilience, your patience, your courage and your kindness. All these difficult things that you've gone through... they help you to see with your Reiki eyes—eyes that always see things from your heart. So count all your challenges as blessings because that's what they are.

MEDITATION WITH THE HARA AND THE FIVE REIKI PRECEPTS

I'd like you to sit comfortably with your palms resting on your lap. Now close your eyes and take a nice, deep, cleansing breathe. Let it out slowly. Imagine with each breath in that the breath is a beautiful light coming in through your nose and filling your body with this light, all the way down to the hara, your lower belly, below your belly button. On the outbreath, imagine this light can expand out through your skin, into your aura and out into the universe. Breathing in... filling your body with healing light, connecting to the hara and breathing out... expanding this light out into the universe. Continue this breathing at your own pace and with each breath in, feel your connection to the hara growing stronger and deeper. With each breath out... feel yourself expanding wider and wider into the universe. Breathing in... connecting to the hara and breathing out... expanding. Breathing in... connecting and breathing out... expanding.

Now, go ahead and return your breathing to normal. Just sit in that beautiful space of energy created with your breath. Energy is inside of you and all around you. Feel the easy flow, the balance and peace. Just for today, do not anger, do not worry, be humble, be honest, be compassionate to yourself and others.

Now I'd like you to bring into your mind an animal

you'd like to offer healing to. I'd like you to bring together the Reiki Precepts and this animal, reflecting on the ways this animal helps you to embody the precepts more fully in your life. For today only, do not anger... do not worry... be humble... be honest... be compassionate. Open your heart to the precepts and to your animal teacher and realize that your animals are always here to show you how to embody these precepts, to inspire you to embody them within yourself.

Open your heart to being present, knowing that you can receive the wisdom of the precepts with the help of your animal. The deeper we go into the teachings of the precepts, the more they can ripple out into our lives. Our animals help us let go of our anger, let go of our worries and live with humility, honesty, and compassion. Our animals help us transform our life so that our life is healing and healing is our life. We're sharing the space in our hearts... remember to keep your heart open so you can always hear their lessons for you.

Now take a moment to thank your animal. When you're ready, setting your intention to finish, take a nice, deep, cleansing breathe and slowly come back...

Conclusion

THROUGH THESE FIVE lessons, we've had a chance to experience the insights of the entire Animal Reiki Practitioner Code of Ethics, including its guiding principles. These principles help us set our intentions for all the good work that we do as Animal Reiki practitioners. We also have reflected on the best ways to work on ourselves, the best ways to work with animals, the best ways to work with the animals' human companions, and the best ways to work in the community. I dearly hope that you feel a strong connection to this code and that you'll find it easy to implement its guidelines, because I know that doing so will not only deepen your own healing journey and help you better connect with the animals and people but also create a more successful and abundant Animal Reiki practice in your life.

Be peace; be light; be love; be Reiki.

Animal Reiki Practitioner Code of Ethics
Developed by Kathleen Prasad

Guiding Principles:

- I believe the animals are equal partners in the healing process.

- I honor the animals as being not only my clients, but also my teachers in the journey of healing.

- I understand that all animals have physical, mental, emotional and spiritual aspects, to which Reiki can bring profound healing responses.

- I believe that bringing Reiki to the human/animal relationship is transformational to the human view of the animal kingdom.

- I dedicate myself to the virtues of humility, integrity, compassion and gratitude in my Reiki practice.

In working on myself, I
follow these practices:

- I incorporate the Five Reiki Precepts into my daily life and Reiki practice.

- I commit myself to a daily practice of self-healing and spiritual development so that I can be a clear and strong channel for healing energy.

- I nurture a belief in the sacred nature of all beings, and in the value and depth of animalkind as our partners on this planet.

- I listen to the wisdom of my heart, remembering that we are all One.

In working with the animals,
I follow these guidelines:

- I work in partnership with the animal.

- I always ask permission of the animal before beginning, and respect his or her decision to accept or refuse any treatment. I listen intuitively and observe the animal's body language in determining the response.

- I allow each animal to choose how to receive his or her treatment; thus each treatment could be a combination of hands-on, short distance and/or distant healing, depending on the animal's preference.

- I let go of my expectations about how the treatment should progress and/or how the animal should behave during the treatment, and simply trust Reiki.

- I accept the results of the treatment without judgment and with gratitude toward Reiki and the animal's openness and participation in the process.

IN WORKING WITH THE HUMAN COMPANIONS OF THE ANIMALS, I WILL:

- Share information before the treatment about my healing philosophy, the Reiki healing system and what to expect in a typical treatment, as well as possible outcomes, including the possibility of healing reactions.

- Provide a clear policy ahead of time regarding fees, length of treatment and cancellation policy, as well as "postponement" policy, should the animal not want the treatment that day.

- Honor the privacy of the animals and their human companions.

- Share intuition received during Reiki treatments, with compassion and humility, for the purpose of supporting their understanding of the healing process.

- Respect the human companion's right to choose the animal's healing journey, selecting the methods, both holistic and/or conventional that he or she deems most appropriate, with the support and advice of a trusted veterinarian.

IN WORKING IN THE COMMUNITY, I HOLD THE FOLLOWING GOALS:

- I model the values of partnership, compassion, humility, gentleness and gratitude in my life and with the animals, teaching by example.

- I work to create professional alliances and cooperative relationships with other Reiki practitioners/ teachers, animal health-care providers and animal welfare organizations in my community.

- I strive to educate my community in its understanding of the benefits of Reiki for animals.

- I continually educate myself to maintain and enhance my professional competence so that I uphold the integrity of the profession.

- I consider myself an ally to the veterinary and animal health community. I work to support their efforts in achieving animal wellness and balance. I honor other disciplines and their practitioners.

INDEX OF MEDITATIONS

About the Author

Kathleen Prasad is founder of Animal Reiki Source and president of the Shelter Animal Reiki Association (SARA). A Reiki practitioner since 1998, Kathleen Prasad formed Animal Reiki Source to teach and share the healing benefits of Reiki for animals and their caregivers. Kathleen's teachings, based on traditional Japanese Reiki techniques and thousands of hours of Animal Reiki experience in the field, represent the world's first specialized, extensive and professional curriculum in animal Reiki.

In Kathleen's nonprofit SARA, volunteer members, guided by Kathleen's teachings, support animal rescue centers around the world. Kathleen has taught Animal Reiki to shelter staff, volunteers and animal lovers in locations around the world such as BrightHaven, Best Friends Animal Society, The San Francisco SPCA, Guide Dogs for the Blind, The CARE Foundation, The Elephant Sanctuary, Animal Haven, The Devoted Barn, Animal Protection Society and Remus Memorial Horse Sanctuary. Kathleen is the author of *Heart To Heart With Horses: The Equine Lover's Guide to Reiki, Everything Animal Reiki* and *Reiki for Dogs*. For more information please visit www.AnimalReikiSource.com or www.ShelterAnimalReikiAssociation.org.

76957583R00080

Made in the USA
San Bernardino, CA
17 May 2018